A MINDSET FOR SUCCESS IN

ENABLING
GENIUS

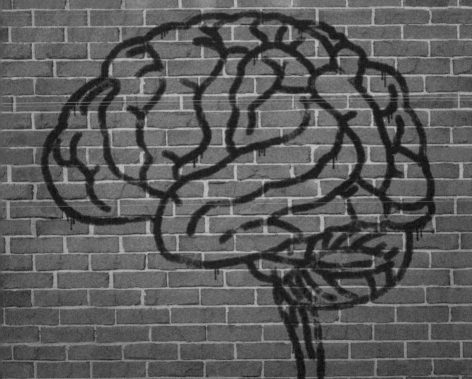

Published by
LID Publishing Ltd.
One Adam Street, London. WC2N 6LE

31 West 34th Street, Suite 7004,
New York, NY 10001, US

info@lidpublishing.com
www.lidpublishing.com

A member of:

BPR
Business Publishers Roundtable

www.businesspublishersroundtable.com

© Myles Downey 2016
© Maxim Belukhin, Sue Coyne, Caroline Cryer, Tamara Cutrín Millán,
James Gairdner, Ian Harrison, Richard Merrick, Andrei Mikhailenko,
Irena O'Brien, Lino Pazo Pampillon, Lena Sobel, Craig Walker
and Simon Williams 2016
© LID Publishing Ltd. 2016

Printed in Great Britain by TJ International
ISBN: 978-1-910649-53-4

Cover and page design: Caroline Li

A MINDSET FOR SUCCESS IN THE 21ST CENTURY

ENABLING GENIUS

MYLES DOWNEY

AND THE

ENABLING GENIUS PROJECT TEAM

LID

LONDON   MONTERREY
MADRID   SHANGHAI
MEXICO CITY   BOGOTA
NEW YORK   BUENOS AIRES
BARCELONA   SAN FRANCISCO

Contents

PART ONE

Enabling Genius

Introduction

There are those who argue, and I am among them, that globally we are in a period of significant transition—a transition, partly facilitated by technology and partly by changing attitudes, from a world in which power is held by a few to a world in which it is held by many. This transition has been described as a shift from "old power" to "new power":

Old power works like currency. It is held by few. Once gained, it is jealously guarded and the powerful have a substantial store of it to spend. It is closed, inaccessible, and leader-driven. It downloads and it captures. New power operates differently, like a current. It is made by many. It is open, participatory, and peer-driven. It uploads and it distributes. Like water or electricity, it's most powerful when it surges. The goal of new power is not to hoard it, but to channel it.
(Source: Harvard Business Review, "Understanding New Power," December 2014, by Jeremy Heimans, CEO of Purpose and cofounder of Avaaz and GetUp, and Henry Timms, Executive Director of the 92nd Street Y and founder of GivingTuesday.)

Old power is an element of a 20th century mindset. Those around the holders of power are expected, and often forced, to comply. Those closer to the source comply because they have had a sniff of power and it's intoxicating and addictive and they want more.

Those further away have fewer resources, are fearful of losing their jobs, and submit. In the world of work, one of the things that marked the 20th century was the drive for efficiency, and it presented us with a useful insight into the limitations of the 20th century mindset. The drive for efficiency has been called "Fordism" after its famous early exponent, Henry Ford. His introduction of the production line transformed manufacturing and started a race for ever-increasing efficiency. Fordism became Total Quality Management, then Business Process Re-engineering (BPR), then Six Sigma, and Lean manufacturing. (Six Sigma is an approach to process improvement in which 99.99966% of all products are expected to be defect free.) Efficiency has brought many benefits and this is not a proposal to undo the good work. However, there are costs; as Michael Hammer, one of the leading exponents of BPR, declared; "We forgot about the people." People end up being secondary, part of the process, and ultimately disposable in service of efficiency. Employee engagement is a major issue in many markets in Western Europe and America, with a significant impact on productivity. And that is not the only cost; efficiency tends to drive compliance. Compliance is the enemy of innovation and creativity. And efficiency has now been taken as close to perfection as can be imagined, so where does improvement and development come from now? The conventional answer is "innovation". But a workforce that has been trained to comply—for years—cannot easily switch on innovation.

This 20th century efficiency model shows up in other ways, too. It works when applied to machines and processes. It does not work for humans. When the same principles are brought into our schools, universities, and hospitals, education and health of the people are no longer being served. Learning to pass exams is not education, it's compliance. So where to next? I would argue that the next frontier is the exploitation, for the greater good, of human ingenuity and creativity: human genius.

New power is a 21st century mindset. An example, again from the world of work, is Linux. Linux is a computer operating system that was created using a model of free and open-sourced development and distribution. Keen users of the system develop upgrades and new software for free and make that available to other users, again for free. This has resulted in a truly massive uptake (it is almost certainly deployed in your smartphone and in the majority of computer games) and also in more innovation and creativity than would be expected in a conventional, controlled, and owned business model. The 21st century mindset is a good thing—unless, perhaps, you are one of the few, a practitioner of Old Power. It's a good thing because of the potential to solve the serious issues the world faces by unchaining the intelligence, creativity, and good will of millions of people. It is also a good thing because it has the potential to deliver more autonomy, more choice, and greater opportunity in all walks of life to individuals like you and me—and others less fortunate. But the transition is incomplete. The battle between old and new power, early skirmishes of which can be detected in the last part of the previous century, will not end in the first part of this one.

My colleagues Richard Merrick and Andrei Mikhaylenko, in their paper, "Context and the Relevance of Genius in the 21st Century," in the second part of this book write:

> *Perhaps the opportunity and need for 21st century genius requires us to ask some powerful questions of ourselves. At a time when we educate and train people to fulfil defined jobs, how do we create the opportunity, space, and permission to pursue ideas that do not have an immediate identified return, but which may be the stuff of genius?*
>
> *When genius is a factor of "messy" human interaction, in an age when we focus on efficiency and risk aversion, how do we make space for the emergence of genius? How do we use the capabilities of technology to increase connection? Can we use that to create the virtual spaces that mirror the informal intensity of the London*

coffee shops? (The London coffee shops of the 1700s became informal meeting places, hubs of innovation, that led to the establishment of the London Stock Exchange, among many other things.)

When it seems highly likely that traditional jobs, including the professions, are going to disappear, how do we define and promote the concept of genius as a vital component of our future wellbeing? If we are to move from the compliance cultures of traditional organizations to the genius cultures needed for our prosperity, what will organizations of the future look like? How do we create the "step changes" that will help us keep pace with the changes already underway?

Genius remains an elusive concept, but its power lies not in its definition, but in our awareness of its existence. Whether it is cause or effect, random or developable, good or bad, is secondary to our need to enable it. The quality of our future demands it.

The requirement to step up our collective performance, to invest in genius, is one of the reasons for writing this book. The second reason is that there is simply an enormous amount of information on human potential in books, research papers, CDs, videos, and online; some of it brilliant, some less so and some impenetrable to the less scientifically minded. In looking at the literature, it quickly becomes clear that individual investigators get very caught up in their particular specialty and do not account for other aspects of the subject. In this book, my co-authors and I have set out to pull together the best research and thinking around excellence from all disciplines, to create an overview, to simplify this, and then to communicate it as well possible. There is yet another reason, perhaps the best one, and this is to spread the profound joy that comes from giving expression to your abilities: your genius.

This book is unusual in that it is very much a joint venture. We have tried to set up the project and write the book on an open commons basis—to be true to our 21st century mindset. It started as the

Enabling Genius Research Project more than two years ago with a small group people from Russia, Canada, Sweden, Spain, and the UK. In the text you will notice that there are some aspects of enabling genius that more than one person writes about. You will even find small disagreements. These have been left in intentionally because they provide different perspectives and opportunities for reflection, perhaps for insight. The editing of the second part of the book, the in-depth articles, has been done with a light hand. My Spanish, Swedish, and Russian colleagues have amazed me with their fluency in English, particularly when writing about a complicated and nuanced topic. To take any idiosyncrasies out would diminish the character of the text. Together we have pulled together research, developed the concepts, written and reviewed each other's works. The book is intended as a device through which you can build your own understanding of genius, of how to enable yourself and others.

The next stage of the enabling genius project is as yet not defined. I imagine getting more people from different specialties involved and doing more research around the "enabling" aspects. As the project progresses, you can find out more and potentially join in by visiting www.enabling-genius.com.

CHAPTER ONE

The Meaning of Genius

Genius, as both an idea and a word, has a long history. And one of the things that marks this history is the changing understanding of it that people, and indeed various societies, have had. I draw attention to this because, in this chapter, I want to show that the current, common understanding is a real and present limitation to human performance. And in so doing open up the possibility for an understanding that might just serve us better.

Very few people get to be called genius—and most of them are dead, which seems a little extreme as a price to pay. I do wonder who gets to confer genius status? Who sets the bar? Is there committee sitting in Geneva? And, whoever and wherever they are, do they only declare genius posthumously?

The prevailing view, outside the world of science, is that genius is the preserve of the few—the very few men, and even fewer women, who stand out as exceptional. In fact, in talking to many people the popular consensus would seem to be that there have only been two geniuses: Einstein and Mozart! Again this makes me wonder. Why would we want to hold onto an idea that genius is for the very few? What or who does that serve?

Perhaps the following anecdote from one of my colleagues in the Enabling Genius Project will shed a little light on what is going on here. She was talking to the human resources director of a large global organization about the Enabling Genius project. Initially there was interest but, when it became clear that the underlying idea was that everyone had genius in them, the director responded immediately with: "We don't need our people to be geniuses, we just need them to do their jobs." I do find it somewhat shocking that an HR director responsible for the wellbeing of some thousands of people should hold such a view. And I am, in equal measure, bemused because I know exactly what was meant. It would seem that society needs people willing to "just do their jobs" and not aspire to anything greater. And many of us are, almost certainly unconsciously, signed up to that idea.

Cannon fodder, factory fodder, wage-slaves, our armed services need people willing to fill the trenches, our factories (whether a manufacturing facility or an accountancy office), need bodies to do the jobs for which we have not yet invented machines to perform. Such a viewpoint is certainly true of the past, but it still holds sway in most quarters today. As a result we have, for instance, education systems that our politicians will proudly tell us are designed to develop people who can find jobs—that is, who will fit into a given slot. And if there are no slots available then you are stuffed because you have been trained to comply, trained to jump through the hoops that we call exams. You have not been trained to be self-reliant—or do I mean you have been trained not to be self-reliant?

What is the primary message from the Adam and Eve fable? Knuckle down and do as you are told—and above all do not seek knowledge, do not explore your potential. The story of Narcissus is equally troubling. Here is a guy, a young man, who is told that he would live to an old age as long as he never knew himself. Looking at one's reflection, I suggest, is an early act in the process of getting to know oneself. The implicit message is that to try and better yourself is vanity and will lead to your death.

However, it is utterly barmy to think that this young man had not seen his reflection before he reached maturity, or had not had the ability to distinguish between himself and his image. In reality, there are deep veins in the strata of our culture that have the effect of limiting our potential by stopping us from exploring it.

I had the following conversation at a conference recently:

Me	*Do you believe that all people have potential?*
Him	*Absolutely!*
Me	*Do you believe that ALL people have genius?*
Him	*No. Absolutely not.*
Me	*So, if I understand you, people have potential but it is limited to somewhere just short of genius?*
Him	*I'll have to think about that.*

Thankfully he was willing and able to question his own assumptions. Many people I speak to are irrevocable against the notion that anyone can be a genius. Often they are people in some position of authority; a headmaster, a church leader, for instance, intent perhaps on preserving their own authority or position. Worse still, most individuals do not believe they are capable of genius: "I am what I am" is the cry, unable to change or develop. No, I don't think so.

In this paradigm where we cannot all be a genius and cannot reach that exalted state or the level of excellence implied, we are doomed to mediocrity or competence at best. So do not even try to reach for genius, do not even imagine it! This is the message given.

If this message is true, it means that the rest of us are not geniuses and, more specifically, do not have the potential to become one.

Which is puzzling because most people are born equipped in pretty much the same way. The same genes, pretty much. Same kinds of bodies, pretty much. And the same number of brain cells and connections between them, pretty much.

But what if this is not true? What if genius is not the preserve of the few, but rather available to all?

A Brief History of Genius

The history and roots of the word "genius" have a tale to tell that explains a little more about how we got ourselves entangled in this self-limiting mess. The word "genius" has its root in Latin. The idea was that each and every person had a guiding spirit, unique to them, whose job was to provide direction and thus to help them progress safely and successfully through life—a genius. A particularly successful person was seen to have a particularly powerful guiding spirit or genius. This idea can be seen in many other cultures. Prior to the Romans, the ancient Greeks had a very similar notion of an invisible being, a Daimon, who watched over a person. According to the Greeks, each person obtained a unique Daimon at birth who guided them, warned them about possible errors but who, interestingly, would never tell them what to do. Never telling their charge what to do suggests a respect for individuality and autonomy that is picked up much, much later by the humanistic movement and, in particular, Carl Rogers' person-centerd approach to therapy. In the Arabia of the past you would find the term Dijinn, or genie, referring to spiritual creatures, also guides, able to interact with people. In these conceptions, genius is a separate entity outside of the self. Then something truly interesting occurred. It seems that the Romans, about two thousand years ago in the time of Augustus, began to use the word to mean talent or inspiration as well, perhaps collapsing the meaning with that of "ingenium," which means innate disposition or talent. The significance is that now genius is understood to be a part of who and what you are, not simply something, a spirit, outside of yourself. The idea of genius as an innate ability really became part of common understanding in the 18th century. This was a big shift in understanding, for if genius is within you then you have some responsibility for and some influence on it. It is also interesting that there is not a strong link to extraordinary performance—everyone had a genius. Some were just more powerful than others.

The link to performance occurred much later. Francis Galton referred to genius in relation to eminence and thus began the connection with excellence. In his book, *Hereditary Genius,* (the title says it all) Galton states, "A man's natural abilities are derived from inheritance ... " He also argued that eminence was rare in a population—the preserve of a few. His central methodology was to count and assess the eminent relatives of eminent men. He found that the number of eminent relatives was greater the closer the connection. The nature-vs.-nurture debate, which we will discuss in detail later on, really begins at this point, and Galton's work is a nature argument: genius is in the genes. His work was much criticized, even his half-cousin, one Charles Darwin, commented thus; "...I have always maintained that, excepting fools, men did not differ much in intellect, only in zeal and hard work, and I still think this is an eminently important difference." Darwin's insistence on the impact of "zeal and hard work" will prove profound, as will be shown in the next chapter. A part of the criticism levelled at Galton was that his work did not account for social status and the resources that would have been available to those more advantaged in this manner—this being the nurture side of the debate.

Genius Today

Galton's ideas about the primacy of hereditary factors remain central to this debate today, and still shape popular understanding. You only have to listen to the language of most sports commentators to see that this is so.

"It's in the genes," they say, inherited, whole and complete, from one's parents. "It's a gift." A gift, from God perhaps, but certainly unearned. Another commentator's favourite is *"She's just a natural!"* I think that if I was that person, the natural—who had dedicated upward of ten years of my life to my sport, forgone holidays, parties, beers, up early in the morning trying to fit in training before rushing off to the day job or my studies, struggling to pay my bills—I would be furious to have that effort, deprivation, and sheer sweat over-looked, even dismissed in such an off-hand manner. Just a natural? No. Of course, and to be clear, genes have a part to play, as we will show later, but the science is more complex than the idea that some people are born geniuses—and more hopeful for those of us who, at first, might not appear as "gifted".

Here's another meaning of genius. Guinness, maker of the famed stout, was and still is, to some degree, famous for advertising. Many were iconic. "My goodness, my Guinness" comes to mind. One campaign ran with the slogan "pure genius". It may be a very Irish use of the word; it is not about the acts or products of a convention-ally defined genius, a person. It refers to something that is perfect for a particular situation, complete in itself, that is the act or prod-uct of an "ordinary" person. A story told, a witty response, a shot at a goal, a sketch that gets to the essence of someone or something. We know it when we see it—pure genius. The Guinness television advertisement showed a pint of the stuff being poured slowly into a glass and settling from the initial creamy brown to a pure black with a cream-coloured head, followed by the words "pure genius". That was the ad, nothing more. In this situation, genius is used to describe a thing and an event. The pint itself. The pouring of the pint. Bringing to mind the moment when you took a draught, when the bitter malted barley taste engulfed your gustatory and olfactory senses. Half the country was salivating. Pure genius, let me tell you.

My colleague on the genius project, Andrei Mikhailenko, gives insight to a further meaning, not completely dissimilar to the last:

Genius was used by Alexander Pushkin in the 19th century meaning of a perfect representation of a certain quality. In this poem (below), the poet's beloved woman appeared before him as the genius of beauty, an ideal manifestation…

"A wondrous moment I remember,
Before me you at once appeared,
A fleeting vision you resembled,
Of Beauty's genius pure and clear.
(From a poem dedicated to Anna Petrovna Kern, written in 1825 by Alexander Pushkin and translated by Julian Henry Lowenfeld.)

The Possibility

So we have genius as an external spirit, as one's innate talents, as one's genetic inheritance, as a thing, an event, a manifestation or a moment. We have genius as the preserve of the few, which traps the rest in mediocrity. Many meanings. A dictionary definition, The Chambers Dictionary 11th Edition, has this to say:

Consummate intellectual, creative, or other power, more exalted than talented, a person endowed with this; the special inborn faculty of any individual; a special taste or natural disposition.

The root is given as Latin, *from gignere, genitum; to beget.* And beget, in turn, means to produce or cause. (Genius is only genius when there is a result.) Of course the bit I like is "the special inborn faculty of any person".

Risking utter pedantry, "genius" is a word. Words are things to which we attach meaning. No word has innate meaning. If words had innate meaning, there would be no need for the roughly

6,500 identified languages that humans have invented—nor the all attendant dialects and regional variations. We frequently relate to words as if they did have innate meaning, which merely results in a stuckness of mind and is a bar to creativity and possibility. As the story here illustrates, the conception of genius is a reflection of a particular society at a particular time. The current concept of genius simply does not serve us as human beings seeking to explore what we are capable of. Worse than that, it actually limits us. There is another possibility and this is the project team's proposition, maybe even a provocation or challenge, which is that genius is available to all.

CHAPTER TWO

Beyond Nature vs. Nurture

Much of the science around human excellence has been explored inside the nature vs. nurture argument—in particular, which of these two has the dominant impact. As an interested observer, it has always struck me as odd that the argument should be so polarized, conducted almost in a right/wrong paradigm. Thankfully recent scientific investigation reveals a little more and shows a more balanced view—that we can influence what we become.

The heart of the nature-vs.-nurture debate, which has been running since Galton coined the phrase in the middle 1800s, is about the relative impact of each of the two components. For clarity, nature embraces all the innate qualities given to an individual, his or her genetic inheritance, while nurture includes all the environmental elements that influence what we become, socially and culturally, including how we were raised and taught, our experiences and relationships.

At one extreme the nature advocates, for example, people with an interest in biological psychology, hold the view that all Behaviours, traits, and characteristics are a result of human evolution. Given that Galton, an early nature protagonist, was a half-cousin of Charles Darwin, this is hardly surprising. At the other extreme are the Behaviourists, some of whom hold the idea that all Behaviours are a result of conditioning. An example is John Locke (1632–1704), a well-known early proponent of the nurture debate and an opponent of the naturists. He took the view that at birth, and indeed when the child was still in the womb, the mind was a *tabula rasa*, a blank slate, and that experience fed it and informed it. This is contrary to the idea that the mind comes with certain knowledge, the naturist position.

For most of the late 1800s and the 1900s, the naturist view held sway. You can see why if you view the issue in the cultural and social climate of the day. As I suggested in the previous chapter, the idea that a person could influence who and what they became is not an idea that would easily find favour with the establishment. This was an era in which people should know their place in society so that there would be labour in the fields and factories, soldiers to be sacrificed in wars, and servants to serve the rich and powerful. Even in the latter part of the past century, the Behaviourists influenced much of management theory—and still do—which is much more about "carrot and stick" and compliance than an individual's intrinsic motivation or about giving people opportunity for growth. The story in the previous chapter about the HR director who did not want geniuses in the organization, but rather people who would "do their jobs," bears testament to this.

The Ten-Year Rule

However, a breakthrough in this thinking, this deadlock, came with the work of Anders Ericsson and his colleagues and was first published in a paper entitled, "The Role of Deliberate Practice in the Acquisition of Expert Performance." Ericsson, a Swede, had previously engaged in a project on memory with William Chase at Carnegie Mellon University. With the help of an unnamed "ordinary" student, they conducted an experiment to develop extraordinary memory. What they found was that, with the right technique and with hours of intensive practice, their guinea pig developed an extraordinary ability to recall more than 80 digits. The biology did not come into it.

Chase and Ericsson reported that "… with an appropriate mnemonic system and retrieval structure, there is seemingly no limit to improvement in memory skill with practice." This was the beginning of a long and productive exploration of the idea of talent for Ericsson, one that he pursued with many collaborators over thirty years.

In 1991 Ericsson, now at Florida State University, conducted what is perhaps his most famous study, aided by two colleagues. The study used violin students from the Music Academy of West Berlin as subjects. Ericsson and company were trying to identify what factors might be causal in outstanding performance. Here's how it was conducted: the students were divided into three groups according to ability. One group comprised the very best, those expected to become soloists with international careers; the next group included those expected to become members of well-known orchestras; and the third was of those who would in all likelihood become music teachers. After extensive interviews, an extraordinary and unexpected finding became clear: without exception the top students had, by the time they reached twenty, put in an average of 10,000 hours of practice over ten years. Without exception. What's more, the second group had put in an average of 8,000 hours and the third group, 4,000. These top students, previously thought to be "gifted," in fact owed their remarkable ability to "deliberate practice", hours of highly intentional, intensive practice.

In their paper, entitled "The Role of Deliberate Practice in the Acquisition of Expert Performance", Ericsson and company wrote:

Only a few exceptions, most notably height, are genetically prescribed. Instead, we argue that the differences between expert performers and normal adults reflect a life-long period of deliberate effort to improve performance in a specific domain.

Different versions of this study have since been conducted, involving many people in many disciplines, all with the same result. Out of this work was born what has now become known as the "the ten-year rule" or the "10,000 hours rule". As Mo Farah, double Gold Medal winner at the 2012 London Olympics, said in an interview with the BBC immediately after winning the final of the 10,000 metres race: "It's just hard work and grafting".

A Musical Genius

Mozart is often upheld as an example of genius and a prodigy (one who demonstrates virtuosity from early childhood, indicating that they are gifted, for they could not have been trained). He was reputedly playing the piano by the age of three, composed his first music at five, and was taken on a tour of Europe at age six.

However, looking into his story is really quite revealing. First of all, his older sister was an accomplished musician who was taught by his father. From his earliest days, therefore, Mozart was hearing music and watching people play and practise. He then started copying his sister's piano playing. His father was a noted musician, composer, and teacher, whose teaching methods were progressive and bring to mind the Suzuki method (not to my mind, but to people who know!). His father set about teaching him the minute he saw Mozart's interest and devoted a large part of his life to his son's talent—with extraordinary results. Here's the thing: given all that input, it would have been surprising if Mozart had been anything less than a genius. And here's another thing: there are those who say that Mozart's early works of composition were really not that good, and that it is only when he reached 17 that he produced great works. That's about ten years.

A Table-Tennis Champion

Matthew Syed tells a similar story in his bestselling book, *Bounce*. Matthew became the number one British table-tennis player at the age of 24 in 1995. The story of how he got there is remarkable for at least two reasons: the thousands of hours of practice and great good fortune. As he tells it, when he was about eight his parents bought a table-tennis table and installed it in their large garage at their home in Reading. His parents were not table-tennis players so there was no family tradition. Also they had a large garage, something not many neighbours had. And Matthew had an older brother, Andrew, with whom to play, which they did, for hours and hours, testing each other and developing new skills. All these factors combined to give Matthew the opportunity for practice.

He says, "Without knowing it, we were blissfully accumulating thousands of hours of practice." Good fortune intervened in the form of their teacher at the local school, Mr Charters, who was responsible for after-hours activities, including, would you believe it, table tennis. And Charters was considered one of the leading, if not the best, English table-tennis coaches. Charters also ran the local table-tennis club, so the boys were invited to play and train there, which they did after school, and on weekends and holidays. It so happened that there was an abundance of talent in the area and the boys trained with local, national, and international champions. Matthew's brother went on to win three national junior titles. And for Matthew, good fortune intervened once more. Arguably the best table-tennis player in history, Chan Xintau married a Yorkshire woman and moved into the locality. He was intent on retiring, but was persuaded to coach Matthew. For many years, Matthew was number one in England, a three-time Commonwealth champion, and competed twice at the Olympics. As he acknowledges, had he been born just one street away, all this might never have happened. The lesson for this book, though, is that of deliberate practice and its impact on excellence.

There are two further stories that are worth referring to in building the picture. Laszlo Polgar, an educational psychologist, decided to conduct an experiment—to train his daughters to become chess Grand Masters. This was no easy task: he was a social chess player at best, had no daughters to train, and was not married nor did he have a girlfriend! He advertised for a wife who would help him with his experiment. In due course he married and produced three daughters and began the training. There is hardly the space here to list all the achievements of all three girls (Olympiads, world titles, competing with and beating the best men). Suffice to say that Judit Polgar, the youngest of the three daughters, is considered to be the best female player of all time and is the youngest person ever to achieve the title of Grandmaster at 15 years and four months.

And then there is Dan McLaughlin, a former commercial photographer from Portland, Oregon. He quit his job in 2010 to take up golf and put in the 10,000 hours of practice. As he set out, he was a very inexperienced golfer who had hardly set foot on a golf course. His goal was to achieve a plus handicap and have the skill set that would allow him to compete on the PGA (Professional Golfers Association) tour. His progress is already surprising—he has a handicap of three—and he is making clear progress toward his goal, which he expects to achieve by 2018. In a way, reaching this goal is irrelevant, for there is genius in the intent itself and in the act of pursuing it.

Genes and Environment

However, as you might have guessed, the story is not quite that simple. The first cloud to cross the early-morning sun for the proponents of the nurture argument was the revelation that the ten-year rule was not quite so definite. In some cases the number of hours was more like 4,000 and for others 22,000 hours. The rule began to look less like a rule.

Then it was observed that if you put someone who had demonstrated an early ability in a discipline alongside someone who had not, and then subjected both to the same training, the person with the ability progressed far more quickly than the other. Not *just* practise, then.

The story now becomes a little more complex and, at first reading, perhaps contradictory. Stefan Holm, a Swedish athlete and exponent

of the high jump, put the hard yards in, did the practice, and per-
fected his technique over many years. Given that Stefan was somewhat stockier than the body type considered ideal for his chosen
discipline, he is a great example of the ten-year rule: he won the
2004 Olympic gold medal—nurture! A different reality is revealed
in the story of Donald Thomas, a college basketball player. Chal-
lenged by some of the athletic fraternity at Lindenwood University
to try the high jump, he strolled up in all the wrong gear, with nothing that could be called a technique, and cleared the bar. Within a
year he was selected to represent the Bahamas and, in 2007 at the
World Championships, beat Stefan Holm into second place. The
thing about Donald Thomas was that he was born with abnormally
long Achilles tendons. These act like springs to propel the jumper
upward—nature! Here's the thing: both athletes in their time were
the best in the world. They just got there by different means.

You may be reading this and thinking that this is the old nature vs.
nurture debate, and there are clearly overtones of that. But there is
more to it. "Versus" means one or the other, not both. Beneath the
argument of the naturist was the idea that genes are a fixed blueprint
or template for what was to develop. And the nurture camp, at the
extreme, denies genetic influence. However, what was not accounted
for was that genes themselves react to their environment. David
Shenk, in his book, *The Genius in All of Us*, says this:

*There is no genetic foundation that gets laid before the environment
enters in: rather, genes express themselves strictly in accordance with
their environment. Everything that we are, from the first moment of
conception, is a result of this process.*

Potently, he also says this:

*Individual difference in talent and intelligence are not predetermined by
genes; they develop over time. Genetic differences do play an important
role, but genes do not determine complex traits on their own. Rather,*

genes and the environment interact with each other in a dynamic process that we can never fully control, but that we can strongly influence.

Lino Pazo Pampillon and Tamara Cutrin Millan, in their article on neuroplasticity later in this book write:

> *After finishing the Human Genome Project in 2003, scientists real-ized that we have approximately 20,500 genes, which is about the same as a mouse, and genes are only part of the story in our individ-ual evolution. A big part is played by so-called 'epigenetic' changes. Epigenetics is concerned with the chemical modifications that alter the expression of the DNA sequence; in effect, this determines how genes are expressed in response to a particular environment. Epige-netic researchers showed that our genetics are like a piano keyboard and, depending on which key you press and how you press it, it will perform different melodies. For some this may sound like a Mozart's concerto, for others like a neighbour who is still learning.*

I get slightly infuriated when attending conferences on topics such as "talent" when the presenter says, "We now know … " and goes on to reveal some research as if it provided a for-all-time valid insight—which conveniently appears to prop up his or her thesis. It is most likely that "what we now know" will be superseded by a new insight before too long. I suspect that there will be a few more twists and turns in the nature vs. nurture debate. Clearly, my interests are in the nurture domain—I want to know more about how human beings reach extraordinary levels of performance and how we can enable that for ourselves and for others.

To get the whole picture, I should tell you about a meta-survey, pub-lished in *Nature Genetics* in May 2015. In this survey of most if not all nature vs. nurture studies (the number of studies was 2,748) con-ducted in the past 50 years, research from 14.5 million sets of twins, measuring 17,804 traits, were analyzed. What the authors of the survey found was that in the development of traits, "The reported heritability is 49%." For our purposes this suggests that, loosely, the environmental aspects—or nurture—account for 50% of what we become. That leaves an awful lot to play with! Moreover, on my reading of the data, there is no account taken of the deliberate effort to develop traits (as opposed to simply being content with what emerges). But, as suggested in this book, we can develop particular traits and that can change the balance of influence over a human lifetime.

Flow

I cannot leave this chapter without talking about an aspect of high performance that is currently the subject of extensive research: in a word, flow. Flow is a mental state. It is different from the hard(er) wiring of genetics in that in any given moment one can be in flow or not. Flow, too, has a long and rich history, which we will look at in depth later in the book.

Many years ago my wife, Jo, gave me as a part of a birthday present a day of flying tuition in gliders. My father had recently passed away and part of my relationship with him, as a boy, had been to accompany him when he went flying from a small club on the fringes of the Dublin airport. He held a private pilot's license until well into his 60s. In his early 20s, during the Second World War, he had flown both Spitfires and Hurricanes, both iconic and extraordinary aircraft. In fact, he had been shot down over Normandy, narrowly escaping death in a burning aircraft. His flying experiences were very much a part of him, and flying itself was therefore a special event. My father, as was the case with many of his generation and upbringing, did not show his emotions or his affection easily, so time spent with him was a unique moment of communication and relationship, albeit in a very male mode. And thus the gift of a day's flying was significant. Gliding is unique in that if a mistake is made, you have no engine to help you correct it. As an example, you lose a lot of height quickly if the craft is out of alignment with the direction of travel. This is likely to happen with a lesser mistake. Bigger ones—well, parachutes are fitted as standard! During the tuition there was frequent and mostly necessary instruction. Mostly necessary—I had had some experience when my father handed me the controls for a few seconds—but some of it distracted me from actually flying. The tutor at some point recognized this. As he was giving the instruction to help me turn the craft around and position it for landing, he stopped himself midsentence as said, *"Oh, just 'effing' fly it!"* And I did. He released me. I had the controls, completely. I was utterly focused and relaxed, at one with the craft. I could feel tiny changes in the air at the tips of my wings and respond before thought intruded. Hands and feet worked ailerons, elevator, and rudder in complete harmony. I cut an absolutely clean turn, losing almost no height. Flow. A moment of genius.

The term "flow" was first used by Mihaly Csikszentmihaly, then head of the department of psychology at the University of Chicago, and made popular in his seminal book, *Flow: The Psychology of Optimal Experience*, published in 1990. He described flow as "Being completely involved in an activity for its own sake. The ego falls away. Time flies. Every action, movement, and thought follows inevitably from the previous one, like playing jazz. Your whole being is involved and you are using your skills to the utmost." Using your skills to the utmost—flow is essential for the highest levels of performance.

An interesting side note: from our investigations, there is emerging research that looks at the impact of flow on deliberate practice. What happens if the practice is executed in flow or not in flow? My current hypothesis is that attending to flow as an integral part of deliberate practice would shorten significantly the time to mastery.

We can influence what we become. And we can, in any act and in any moment, perform well or poorly depending on our state of mind, whether we are in flow or not. The mental state of flow is available to all. In this "story of genius" there are at least three key variables; our genetic inheritance, the environment that surrounds us, and our mental state. Two of these we can influence directly. The idea that "I am what I am" is simply without substance.

CHAPTER THREE

The Propositions: a New Meaning for Genius

The previous two chapters have, I hope, set the scene for this chapter—a more compelling, provocative and, frankly, useful understanding of genius. An understanding that we hope encourages people to explore the upper reaches of their capabilities. As I have tried to show, genius has been understood over many years, centuries in fact, in a number of different ways. The current, prevailing understanding is still founded in what can now be seen as a fallacious argument: genes dictate what you become. No, genius is not simply a function of what you are born with but, much more significantly, what you make of what you are born with. It is clear, too, that the path to genius is available to all. (Key elements of this path are, as I will show, deliberate practice and how to design it.) Then, looking at what Csikszentmihalyi calls "flow", we see that there is a mental state in which people achieve extraordinary levels of performance. No feat of genius can be achieved if the performer is not in flow for periods of time. And flow is distinctly available to all. Of course, getting into flow is not yet a science, more of an art, but there are clear steps for that particular process, which we will explore.

Proposition One: Genius is Available to All

Given that the meaning, or more accurately the understanding, of any word shifts, no one gets the right to define it. The intent here is to make a case for an understanding that serves us better, which is more fitting to our needs and aspirations. The first proposition—of five altogether—is the simplest and most obvious, and you will already have worked it out. *The proposition is that genius is available to all.* As Buckminster Fuller said in a tribute to Maria Montessori, the famous Italian physician and educator:

All children are born geniuses. 9,999 out of every 10,000 are swiftly, inadvertently degeniused by grownups.

Genius is a slightly less hackneyed word than potential, which has lost its potential (forgive me): it drifts by in conversation without causing anyone to think. Genius, I propose, refers to the innate ability of each and every individual—all the resources, skills, abilities, and capacities that are part of being human. Genius is the uninhibited expression of those resources.

Genius is an intent and way of engaging that I can awaken in myself and inspire in others, to allow this instrument—me, you—with all our capabilities and limitations, to be expressed in a given moment. Genius is intent in action.

Genius is a provocation. By comparison, "to be my best self" contains a get-out clause, as in "Well, I guess my best self just is not very great!" "To be my best self" is a notion stuck in the idea that "genes dictate" and that one's potential is limited to hereditary succession. But to intend genius has no such escape route. To intend genius is to give oneself an on-going, everyday challenge.

Genius is joyous, healthy, holistic, creative, generative, life enhancing, and affirmative. It is being "unstuck," inhabiting your own authority and autonomy, and is self-actualizing. Genius is a choice available to each and every one of us.

Proposition Two: Each Person Can Develop a Unique Individual Genius

We propose that each person can develop a *unique individual genius*. As will become clear in the later chapter on Identity, in which I suggest that who we are is not set in stone but is changeable, a unique individual genius is something that we choose for ourselves. It is not predetermined by a deity or by one's genes. One of my colleagues on this project, Irena O'Brien, put it this way:

The optimal way to develop genius is to find what we're naturally good at (genes), and then nurture that.

Choosing a discipline for which we are not well matched is going to make the job harder—if not impossible. We have not yet come across research that sheds light on just how close the match needs to be, but I can only assume that the better the fit, the greater the resulting excellence. There is a quote that has been attributed to Einstein, but I can find no evidence that he actually said it. Nevertheless, it is appropriate for us here:

Everybody is a genius. But if you judge a fish by its ability to climb a tree, it will live its whole life believing that it is stupid.

It is possible that we may develop more than one genius and I will address that in the next proposition. The idea of a single unique individual genius is that in being focused on one discipline, we are much more likely to achieve excellence. The first task is to choose our unique individual genius. This might start with how a person defines himself or herself: musician, tennis player, lawyer, teacher, or salesperson. Or even something more archetypal, such as a leader, servant, or religious/spiritual guide. Another starting point might be what genuinely interests or fascinates us. Then the task is to define how we, with all our unique gifts, best approach that discipline, craft or skill set. And each person will approach it differently—this is the essence of unique, individual genius. Then comes the task of developing our chosen genius.

I have had a number of roles and phases in my working life: architect, tennis coach, business coach, trainer of coaches, company director, business owner, author—with varying degrees of success. A few years ago, in 2011, I left a business, The School of Coaching, which I had previously sold, without a clear idea of what I was going to do next. The only clarity I had was that I did not want to start another school. I had done it, it was successful and fun, but it was time for something new. My strategy—I can only call it that in retrospect—was to engage in a variety of projects as a way of working through my options. One project, the creation of an automated coaching system now called Enable, emerged as a strong candidate for my attention. So I put time, money, and effort into it.

After two years it was going somewhere, not nowhere, but very slowly and I was spending most of my time doing things that I was capable of (just), but which gave me little pleasure: trying to recruit a managing director, searching for a reliable IT firm to develop the platform, and speaking to investors. It was like trying to drive a car in second gear on the motorway with the brakes on—handbrake and footbrake. In something close to desperation, I arranged a conversation with my coach, Cliff Kimber. Gradually the light shone through. The first insight was that the activities that I was spending my time on were not consistent with my primary skill set or what I would now call my unique individual genius. What became clear was that I was being driven by a received idea that in order to be successful I had to build capital value—grow a business that was worth a chunk of money—and this was driving behaviours and actions that I could do but was not truly great at. With more talk and reflection I began to understand that my unique individual genius was as an author. There was a point when I looked at my diary and saw my days filled with meetings, conferences, training events, and telephone calls—but no writing was scheduled. My diary was inconsistent with my genius. Now I keep Tuesdays and Fridays for writing. The idea of "author" expands to writing the coaching scripts for the automated coaching system and then to any idea, anything that might be termed intellectual property. As soon as an idea takes shape, I form partnerships with others who develop it, deliver it, or take on some aspect that is not part of my unique individual genius.

McKinsey and Company, the much-respected global strategic consultancy, uses a concept that reflects this idea in relation to the development of their consultants. One has to be very competent in a whole variety of areas—knowledge and skills—in order to succeed in the firm. And to excel and indeed differentiate oneself, you need to have a "spike": an aspect in which you are outstanding. This is something you identify and then nurture over time.

In my experience, not many people think about themselves as having genius. Mostly we fall into careers or jobs as a function of the expectations around us (which is why I studied architecture), our abilities, or simply the opportunities that are available locally. I have yet to met the career advisor who thinks of his or her charges in terms of their genius.

At different stages in life, we may be called to develop different unique individual geniuses. Some careers, like those of professional sports players, only last a few years, a decade if they are lucky. And so they are forced to develop new careers. Some have done this really well. Sebastian Coe, now Lord Coe, the middle-distance runner and Olympic gold medallist among many other achievements, went on to lead the hosting of the very successful Olympic Games in London in 2012—a completely different discipline. As people live longer, the opportunity to develop genius in a number of areas becomes even greater and, arguably, more important. As we progress through the ages and stages of life, our strengths and abilities change. The apprentice becomes the craftsperson, who then becomes the master craftsperson with a broader perspective and apprentices now in his or her care. And then there is the possibility of eldership. There is the potential for a new and different unique individual genius in each phase.

Proposition Three: Each Person Can Develop Genius in any Discipline, Craft, or Skill

We also propose that you can develop genius in any discipline, craft, or skill. This is likely to be an aspect of my life that I have a great interest in or a need to develop in order to survive or thrive. I cannot be a great independent management consultant if I cannot sell, for example, so I might approach my development as a salesperson to find my genius in it. Or I may find that I am involved in a business life that does not inspire me but one that I cannot for whatever reason, get out of. I may then choose to develop another aspect of my life for the fulfilment and learning that would ensue.

Simon Williams, a project team member, wrote this:

My guitar playing, cycling, and this genius project are all examples for me of areas I am trying to develop that are not my day job but inform, support, and develop my day-to-day consultancy and leadership roles. I would be incomplete without doing both. My day job would be much the poorer if I could not do them. And in years to come, as I step back from my company, they will become my primary focus.

As a part of the Enabling Genius Project, I set up my own personal genius project as a laboratory to test what we were uncovering in the research. That project is to get back to playing competitive tennis. At the time of writing I am 55 and there is a very strong amateur tournament set up in which I am planning to compete. In my childhood and into my mid-twenties, I played competitive tennis and was relatively good. When I tell you that most of my tennis was played in Ireland, you will understand what "relatively" means! In the early days there was no coaching to speak of, and no supporting structure for people who really wanted to develop their game—it was mostly a social pursuit. However, we had a kind of "golden era" with one home-grown tennis player, Sean Sorensen, ranked just outside the top 100, and one import, Matt Doyle, who was ranked within the top 80. My best tennis was played with Matt on one of only two indoor courts in Ireland, when he was passing through Dublin and was desperate for someone, anyone, with whom to practise. I looked like I knew what I was doing on the tennis court and my sponsorship from Slazenger made sure that I looked the part, too. I think this was why I ended up playing a member of the visiting Harvard Yale tennis team in the first round of the Irish Open in 1985 (Steve Poorman if I recall correctly). I am suggesting here that there was some fixing of the draw to get something that looked like a match on the center court for day one of the championships. I played the best match I had ever played, until the second half of the second set, when two things happened. I lost my focus after a bad line call (I can still see the serve in my mind's eye) and fell out of flow. And my hangover kicked in with a vengeance. I had played in an inter-club competition the day before and our team had won. This necessitated a visit to the clubhouse bar, obviously, and, well this was Dublin in the 80s.

The next day there was a by-line in the Irish Times written by tennis correspondent Vera McWeeney, something of a family friend, which began with, "Myles Downey, the still-promising junior … " I was 23! In short, I had some ability that was never quite fulfilled, but occasionally and frustratingly glimpsed. This was long in the back of my mind to the extent that about ten years ago I made myself a promise to take a sabbatical and play competitive tennis—buy an old red London bus and convert it into a mobile home and head off to France! (There is a great tournament set up there.)

Two years ago the phone rang and a tennis coach, now a member of the genius project team, Craig Walker, introduced himself, saying that two people in the previous 24 hours had mentioned my name as an Inner Game coach and someone he might profit from speaking to. Craig works at a tennis center ten minutes from where I live in London and has a deep understanding of both the technical and psychological sides of tennis. My genius project began. Every aspect of my game has been examined. We changed every stroke.

Two months after we began the project I could hit the ball—but I had no idea where it was going to go! The old form died away and a new form emerged.

The process started with a question from Craig: "As a tennis player, what is your signature?"

I kind of understood but asked in return: "What do you mean, my signature?"

"How do you play your best tennis? What does your best tennis look like?"

We spoke about the way I played and the tennis players with whom I identified the most. My unique individual genius as a tennis player became clearer and we deliberately designed my practice on the basis of it. I now play tennis in the modern way (I was brought up on grass courts with wooden rackets) and am hitting the ball harder, with more weight and with more accuracy, than when I was playing tournaments in my 20s. It is unlikely, I reluctantly acknowledge, that I will become the world's over-55 singles champion. But one thing I am certain of, or as certain as one can be about anything, is that sometime very soon I will take to the court and play with freedom, power, creativity, and accuracy and thus, for a period of time—a game, a set, a match—body and mind will be as one and utterly self-expressed. Such joy!

Tennis is not my primary activity, not my current unique individual genius, but I can approach it in the same manner as if it were, with a similar intent to develop and exploit my genetic inheritance and whatever abilities I have developed since birth. And even if there is some inherent limitation or disability, even if I am not a great match for a particular discipline, craft, or skill set, I can still approach it with the intent that I would bring to developing my unique individual genius. And that, I suggest, is genius.

I have noticed that many people who achieve excellence in one domain are often very good in one or two others. I think it may be a real help, as the learning from one discipline can shed light on the other. This can show up in fairly obvious skills and abilities: the ability to concentrate, to get into flow, self-confidence and willingness to learn being just a few. More subtly, ways of engaging in activities, beliefs about oneself and characteristics like self-confidence can be transferred from one discipline to another. As I engaged in the tennis project, I realized that when I was competing in my youth I had a very simplistic notion about how to win: hit the ball harder, preferably to a place on the court where my opponent was not. There was a strong parallel in my business life in which, as I described, I was not succeeding in the manner I desired—I did not know how to win. As I learned how to win in tennis, there were considerable lessons that I began to apply to my business. Two examples are the real clarity about what "winning" means for me in business and a simplified approach or strategy more aligned with my goals.

Proposition Four: Moments of Genius Are Available to All

The next proposition is that moments of genius are available to all. Moments of genius are spontaneous, mostly unplanned events. You are walking down the street and an insight occurs. Genius. You're having an early-morning shower and a solution to a problem that has been bothering you pops into your mind. A friend of mine was driving in London's West End, looking for a parking space, and spotted a person getting into a parked car. He positioned himself to take the parking spot. Another car drew up alongside with an irate and aggressive-looking man behind the wheel. He lowered his window and said that the owner of the parked car had promised him the spot. My friend instantly responded with a warm smile and *"Let's toss a coin for it."* The situation was instantly defused—spontaneous, unplanned, and unrehearsed. Uninhibited self-expression. Genius. And he won the toss.

"It's like this," another friend of mine, Peter, observed. "Anytime you're walking down the street, wherever you are going, whatever you are doing, your genius is by your side. The only questions is— are you open to it?"

Knowing your genius is "by your side" means that you can, to a degree, plan for moments of genius (I know I said "mostly unplanned" in the opening sentence of this paragraph). Frequently, when I am faced with a problem, I do not seek to solve it in one go. I might create a mind-map and just leave it on my desk. I may come back to it a few times and add some notes. I trust that when the moment is right, often in the shower or when I am running, a solution pops into my mind.

Proposition Five: People Can Work Together in a State of Collective Genius

The fifth proposition is that there is a state of *collective genius*. This is when a group of individuals comes together in a state of flow and delivers something extraordinary. While this most often happens in situations where there is an immediate need to perform, such as sports or the performing arts, it can also happen in teams at work. Some years ago I did some work with a colleague, Judith Firman, with a team that was in the process of launching a bank. They had a sort of mantra, which was about "dancing with customers". Judith suggested that they should learn to dance together. This was initially met with some resistance but, after a while, Judith prevailed and they started learning to dance. At the launch party, in front of a few hundred staff, the leadership team performed the dance and brought the house down—it had been kept a secret. However, apart from the drama, it was really noticeable that, after the dance practice, conversations were more fluent, interruptions were purposeful and often challenging, and the group began to facilitate its own conversations. In these moments the group had little need of the facilitators, Judith and me, and operated with sensitivity, speed, and decisiveness.

On one occasion they elegantly solved a problem in 50 minutes that the board of the parent company had not resolved in five hours the day before.

This is such an immense topic in its own right that we are simply bringing it to the attention of our readers as a possibility. In the second part of this book, Andrei Mikhaylenko and Lena Sobel's article develops this thinking. Lena writes:

> *A high-performance team needs to be in flow, the state where the individuals are fully immersed in a feeling of energized focus, full involvement, and enjoyment in the process of the activity. A team in flow can be characterized by the ease and sense of fulfilment and purpose that the participants enjoy, as well as a perfect notion of goals and purpose. Problems are there to be solved and new ideas keep emerging. In the state of flow, everything seems possible. Teams achieve results with fewer resources, time, money, and people than everyone thought possible, team members included. Individuals build on each other's ideas and contributions and are more or less single-minded in the pursuit of solutions and results. And at the same time, open to contributions from other teammates.*

The Pillars of Enabling Genius

It is our intent to make the information we have pulled together in this book as useful and pragmatic as possible. But given the vast amount of information on genius and its near cousins—excellence, high performance, talent, and neuropsychology—all the models and theories, and all the brilliant people who have something to say, we hope that a large element of our work will make the territory more comprehensible. That means simplifying and cutting things down to the essentials.

When thinking about your own or another's genius, an early place to look for direction in enabling and developing genius might be this model. It is in this spirit that I introduce the Pillars of Enabling Genius.

Pillars, in the architectural sense, are the components of a building that hold it up. But they are not the whole building. The Pillars of Enabling Genius do not collectively represent a model for the whole of genius and how one enables it. That domain is too great to be captured in any one model, I suspect. The pillars are, in the view of the project team, the principle ideas. The proposition here is that the stronger each of the Pillars, the more likely one is to be a genius.

The Pillars of Genius

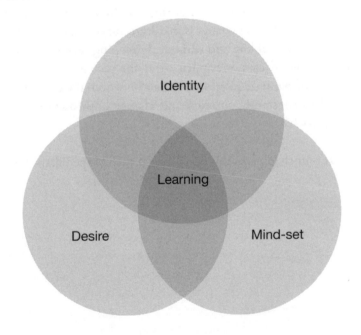

Since this model first emerged, there have been two changes. The first is that I had the word "drive" where you now see "desire". The distinction I am making here is linguistic and goes beyond any dictionary definition. I am making the distinction to bring clarity.

The word "drive", it seems to me, suggests a strong masculine energy, single-minded and goal-driven, brooking no obstacle. I think the world is too messy and changing and too open to the needs and intentions of others for such an idea to be always appropriate or useful. "Desire" suggests that one is awake to and tolerant of the needs of others, to the changing nature of the environment or context within which one is desiring. It suggests a more emergent, changeable, purposeful energy. Desire, then, as used in this model, embraces both ideas, both masculine and feminine energies.

Initially drive, now desire, was at the center of the model. It was an instinctive move—surely everything starts with motivation? However, the more I thought about it and the more I investigated genius, the more I began to realize that learning should be at the center. The first justification for this change is that learning and development are fundamental to enabling and without developing each of the pillars in oneself, genius cannot happen. And the second is that almost every story of genius requires individuals on whom the title has been bestowed to constantly question and change both themselves and their approach.

The next four chapters of this book look at each of the Pillars in turn.

CHAPTER FOUR

Identity

Identity has a vital function: in order to have a relationship with another, I need to have a sense of whom I am relating to, I need to get a handle on him or her. This means that, within parameters, I can have some certainty about the person who shows up day-to-day and make agreements and plans with that person. With some people, like those I meet when walking the dog, maybe all I need is a first name. With others, if we are to do something significant together, like get married, I need to know a bit more. I also need to be able to get some kind of a handle on myself too. It would be difficult if I woke up every day to a different me.

Internal dialogue:

- *What will I have for breakfast today? Cereal?*
- *No, not cereal—that's just not me. I'll have fruit.*
- *Yesterday I hated fruit! And anyway, I didn't buy any!*
- *And I have not even begun to think about what to wear!*

You would go mad starting over every day.

More immediately relevant to this book is that identity, our sense of self, is essential to our individual emergence as a human being for it is on this base that we develop ourselves, promote ourselves, and thus take our place in our communities. Having a better understanding about the nature of identity is a prerequisite to beginning to think about and develop a unique individual genius.

Identity has many guises. People ask at a party, "What do you do?" They try to place your accent, and try to establish if you are married. Your sexuality. Your age. Your religion. Your wealth. Your place in society. All in order to find out something about whom you are. And Identity has many close cousins: I, me, myself. Person, self, personality. Then there is the ever-present "I" in our speaking and thinking, which demands examination for it is this that we frequently relate to as the seat of our self. But it is not so simple, for identity is elusive both as a thing and as a concept.

As a concept, theologians and religious leaders of every persuasion, psychologists, neuroscientists, anthropologists, and philosophers, to name a few categories of interested parties, have through many centuries spoken and written about it, often expounding very different ideas. But there is little that can be said with absolute certainty, for there is no scientific evidence for the self.

As a thing, well, we have such a strong sense of our selves and our identity that we do not often question it or reflect upon it, other than the occasional moment, as when looking with awe at the stars in the night sky, we ask ourselves, "Who am I?" I just am, it's a given. This given-ness finds an echo in the language: "Just be yourself"—from my observation, not always a good idea! The exhortation typically slips by the target, but it really demands a question: "how would I do that—'be myself'?" Another common expression is this: "It's just not me," maybe said when trying on an item of clothing. Well, which you? The one who parties, the one who goes to work, the one who takes care of the children? If we each can develop a unique individual genius, then these questions require a better understanding, if not answers.

The "Pearl" View of Identity

The received notion is that there is a part of me, my identity, at my core. The dictionary definition supports this: *Identity: the state of being the same; sameness; individuality; personality; who or what a person is. From idem; the same. (The Chambers English Dictionary 12ᵗʰ Edition.)* The state of being the same. A part of our intuitive understanding of identity is to think of it as that element of the self that has persisted through the years. We meet old childhood or school friends and immediately recognize them through a certain configuration of facial parts, posture, way of speaking, or attitude. There will have been changes, of course, no one survives the ravages of time intact, but there is something the same: who they are, their identity. In this understanding, identity—as with a stick of rock, the confection you might buy at the seaside, which has a word, the name of the resort town where it was bought perhaps, that persists running through the center as you crunch your way down the stick—has a core that remains the same over time. This has been labelled "the pearl view," the jewel at the center of the oyster.

But there is an insurmountable problem with the pearl view— nobody has found the pearl! There is no place in the body or mind where the self is located. Even the part of neuroscience community that has been looking at this has pretty much given up on the search. Scientists cannot identify a location in the brain that might be labelled a "unified center of consciousness," a self.

The Construct View of Identity

The primary competing view is that of identity as a construct. A construct is something that is put together in one's mind, as opposed to a real object—a mental model. The suggestion is that our identity is something that emerges as a function of what we inherit physically and mentally, what we absorb from our family environment, our social environment, and from all our experiences and memories. Memories are different from the experiences that gave birth to them. What we retain, delete, or distort from the original experiences, our memories, become a part of how we think of ourselves. Add to this the unique manner in which we construe all of this. How we put it together, understand it, and hold it. Unconsciously, we are constructing an identity, a sense of self, which will survive and, with luck, thrive in its environment—that is *fitting*, to borrow from Darwin.

Julian Baggini, philosopher and author, in his book, *The Ego Trick*, explores these two competing ideas. His argument favours the construct concept and, with others, puts the label "Bundle Theory" on it. He suggests our sense of self emerges from our thoughts and perceptions but that there is no "control center," no pearl. This is the "trick" of the title of the book. He uses the word trick not as a magician might but as a mechanic would: "So if your car needs repair and the mechanic can't get the part, he might have a 'trick' that gets the car working as normal anyway."

He goes on to say:

There is no single thing that comprises the self, but we need to function as though there were. As it happens, the mind, thanks to the brain and body, has all sorts of tricks up its sleeve that enable us to do this. Because it succeeds, selves really do exist. We only go wrong if we are too impressed by this unity and assume that it means that underlying it is a single thing. But self is not a substance or thing, it is a function of what a certain collection of stuff does.

Or, as the psychologist Carl Rogers said (there will be more about him later) of "self concept":

... the organized, consistent, conceptual gestalt composed of perceptions of the characteristics of 'I' or 'me' and the perceptions of the relationships of the 'I' or 'me' to others and to various aspects of life, together with the values attached to these perceptions. It is a gestalt that is available to

awareness though not necessarily in awareness. It is a fluid and changing gestalt, a process, but at any given moment it is a specific entity.

The word gestalt in psychology means: "an organized whole that is perceived as more than the sum of its parts." This is a more philosophical proposition than scientific. That said, from the work that the Enabling Genius team has done, identity as construct has the most weight behind it and, from a purely practical place, is most useful in enabling genius, for it takes us away from identity as a fixed thing and suggests that it is something that emerges over time and is far more plastic than commonly thought and that can, to a degree, be shaped.

Personal Construct Theory and Construing

Suggesting that identity as construct "is more useful" takes me to George Kelly, originator of Personal Construct Theory and an arch pragmatist. In the early 1930s, with a PhD in psychology, he found himself in Kansas. This was post-Depression America and the local population was desperate, suffering terrible poverty, and with little opportunity to take themselves out from it. Kelly felt himself to be ill-equipped for the task of supporting them but, in listening to his clients and giving them his interpretations of their various situations, he saw that, while his interpretations were sought, it was the sense that people made of them that helped. And if this new sense also helped them find a new way forward, it was most appreciated.

This observation that people made sense of things for themselves was developed in Kelly's theory as the idea of "the man as scientist," with himself as the subject. It brings to mind the quote in Plato's *Apology* and attributed to Socrates, *"The unexamined life is not worth living."* Maybe the "is not worth living" bit is a little harsh and even righteous, but as a rhetorical flourish, it has drama. It was Kelly's intent that we should examine ourselves and our lives, and this means examining our constructs. This in turn means examining and arranging the facts of one's experience—creating the construct—and then testing that construct in real life. If the results that follow are aligned with what the construct suggests, then all is, literally, well. If not, we can re-examine the facts and modify the construct.

And this takes us to "construing", a term Kelly used. In Trevor Butt's book, *George Kelly, the Psychology of Personal Constructs,* Butt says:

It is important to think of construing as something we do, rather than construct as things we have ... Perhaps it is more accurate to think of construing as questioning.

This is a significant distinction because it suggests that construing is a process and, importantly, an on-going one. "Have" suggests something more permanent, more difficult to change. A process, on the other hand, suggests that the construct can shift, change, or develop. Many of the constructs that I operated from as a child are unlikely to serve me as an adult.

Max Weinreich, a linguist who, among many things, was the professor of Yiddish at City College, New York, gives the definition: "A person's identity is defined as the totality of one's self-construal, in which how one construes oneself in the present expresses the continuity between how one construes oneself as one was in the past and how one construes oneself as one aspires to be in the future." The definition is fine but the last part of it adds to our understanding of how to develop one's unique individual genius—"as one aspires to be in the future". For many, such aspiring will be pretty unconscious. For those intent on developing genius, awareness and clarity in one's aspiration is a point of leverage.

All this suggests that as time passes or circumstances change, I can reinvent myself. Reinventions most obviously occur as people pass through different ages and stages in their lives. The mother who brought up the children goes back to work. The former executive takes on a nonexecutive directorship and a role in a charity. Or the change can be more dramatic and fundamental. I recall my mother telling me about a family friend who worked for years as an accountant and then, surprising everyone, retrained as a lawyer when in his 50s.

Maxim Belukhin, in his article that focuses on the disillusion than can arise from sticking with a version of oneself that is inauthentic, writes:

> *Herminia Ibarra (professor of leadership and learning at Insead Business School) suggests ... [an] approach: 'shaping and revealing the self through testing. Learning from direct experience to recombine old and new skills, interests, and ways of thinking about oneself and to create opportunities that correspond to that evolving self.' This approach is based on the idea that we can have millions of possible selves. All we need is to start a very committed journey through daring, safe investigations in which we can see what works for us. In turn, it is important to be aware of how we feel when we present a fake self. After the experiments we can shape several possible selves and switch to one with far better chances for success and happiness.*

My personal construct system is instrumental in what I choose to do and how I show up in life. If this is malleable, and it is, then I can, with care and attention and some patience, shape my "bundle". I can bring to the fore various aspects of my bundle according to the needs of a situation, or better, in line with my intent and aspirations. In the context of Enabling Genius, my unique individual genius is a construct and a part of my personal construct system (I have other constructs; I am constantly construing). I may find that I am not clear about what my unique genius is, or I may discover that my construct is out of date or simply misconstrued. If so I can reinvent, I can reconstrue. Identity shape-shifts—a genius does this consciously.

Authenticity and Continuity

This brings up a question about authenticity. If I can simply modify my construct, how can it be really me? This is in part answered by the construct theory itself: there is no real you, merely the bundle doing its trick. Another part of the answer is that an element of anyone's bundle is our memories and these that provide us with a sense of continuity and indeed connectedness. Our memories allow us to connect with the child we once were and know that one is still that same person—even though every cell in our body has changed. In the quote by Carl Rogers earlier, he used the words: *". . . organized, consistent, conceptual gestalt . . . "*

Ian Harrison, in his article on identity, writes:

> *There are, I think, three statements with which most people would agree, regarding our experience of identity. Each one of these is helpful in the context of enabling genius. Whichever view you hold regarding the nature of the self, each of us has a strong enough experience of identity to reach one of the most simple and the most profound statements possible: 'I am.' There is a me and I am unique. In whatever way my self is constructed, however much of myself exists at conception and to whatever extent I am shaped by psychosocial experiences—I am, and no one else is quite like me.*
>
> *Secondly, and equally undeniably, I change. I am shaped by my experience of life and I express myself differently in different contexts. Finally, whether or not science ever identifies a core self, I remain recognizable. That is to say that, as I change, develop, and grow there is a progressive consistency. If you were to meet a close friend after many years apart you would perceive them to have changed greatly and yet you are almost certainly going to recognize certain traits of character from all those years ago. I am. I change. I remain recognizable.*

However, the notion of authenticity also conceals a dangerous trap. The idea of a fixed me, an unchanging core is, to some, quite comforting—it means I cannot really change and therefore don't need to bother. As a coach, I have on many, many occasions worked with senior people in leadership positions who have a need, either for their own reasons or because the organization for which they work demands it, to examine their leadership approach. In this context I hear about authenticity; the change "must be authentic". There is truth in that, but, in more than half these cases, what I was really being told was that the person was unwilling to change. To be fair, there have been many understandable reasons behind the unwillingness:

- Fear of failure: "I will never be as good as the previous leader."
- Fear of success: "If I do this well, then I will have to spend even more time away from home."
- Fear of change: "What if I can't change?"
- Fear of the cost of change: "I am stressed enough already without taking this change on."

And more. But it is the death of genius.

So, in the context of enabling genius, how might we think about authenticity?

While the self is a construct, that does not mean that it does not exist. It is a bundle composed of, among other things, your experiences, memories, values, ethnicity, religion, education, and so on. So do what you feel predisposed to do, probably something you have been exposed to—build on the existing foundation. Do what your inheritance suggests. Do what interests you. Kelly's rule is to test the construct in real life. If the results that follow are as envisaged, well and good. If not, re-examine the facts and reconstrue.

I remember as an insecure teenager asking my elder sister, Eve, if I should wear a particular deep yellow pullover—would it be me? Her response was wonderful: "If you wear it, it will!" Of course, I learned over time that yellow was really not my colour given my

Irish complexion, but walking around Dublin looking like a traffic light stuck on amber did have its moments. My point here is that identity is something that develops, or for those interested in genius, is developed, and that trying on new clothes, new ways of being or doing and making mistakes is a useful, expanding, and enhancing exercise.

Multiple Geniuses

The Enabling Genius team's second proposition is that a person can develop their genius in any craft or discipline in addition to their unique individual genius: multiple geniuses. As an example, some years ago I needed to put more attention on my sales activities after a period of writing. In thinking about it, I realized that my internal approach needed to shift, as writing requires a different energy than selling. I asked myself a series of questions to see if I could identify the sales genius therein and bring it to life. The questions included: "What's his name? What kind of energy does he have? What is his dominant attitude? How does he dress? What music does he listen to?" In answering these questions, I brought my sales genius to life and had new energy with which to pursue my sales goals. I also clarified my approach so that I was more focused and, therefore, closer to being in flow when in sales situations.

It is almost certain that the unique genius that a person brings to each of their separate activities would be different. That's to say each genius would draw on different elements of the bundle and bring a different quality to the fore. My tennis-playing genius is quite different from my coaching genius. The first is more aggressive and intent on winning the match, while the second is more passive, receptive, compassionate, and intent on my clients getting the outcome they desire. Different parts of my nature—different bundles—for different activities. It would not do, but might be quite entertaining if my tennis genius showed up while I was coaching. I said earlier that, as a tennis player, I did not have a good idea about how to win. A part of the problem was that I was teaching tennis at the same time I was playing competitively and my coach genius did show up in matches: I would find myself hitting the ball to my opponent, not away from him. This was not a winning strategy.

The idea of multiple geniuses finds a parallel with an element of Roberto Assagioli's thinking in the psychological approach that he developed, Psychosynthesis: Sub-personalities. Assagioli was an Italian, born in Florence in 1888 and much of his approach was developed after the Second World War. His approach to psychoanalysis was based on Sigmund Freud's, in which he was trained, but he felt that there was something missing from the Freudian method, that it was too reductive in application and was derived from working with people who were suffering rather than from those who were healthy, coping adults. Above all, it did not account for the creative and positive aspects of the human being. Psychosynthesis, as it developed, was more holistic than the Freudian approach and had a spiritual component. What is relevant here is that Assagioli suggested that each individual has numerous sub-personalities. To illustrate, my wife, Jo, used to hate meeting me in town while I was working. She said that I was not the same person as I was at home, as if putting on a suit changed me into someone else. At first I did not understand and did not, I confess, pay much attention to the feedback. But it gradually dawned on me that in this matter, as in most things, she was right. When we met in the office I was in a particular sub-personality, one that was for the most part appropriate to that specific environment. On most days I would have the journey home to gradually discard the mantle of a business owner and manager and adopt that of husband. When we met in or close by the office I did not have the time, or frankly, the awareness, to go through the subtle shift required.

Sub-personalities are sometimes archetypes: mother, father, child. apprentice, master. teacher, student. Every archetype will also be unique and personal; the way I played out "father" was an expression of myself, my bundle. Then there are sub-personalities that are very specific to individuals. I possess a number: there's one in particular that wears an Aran sweater, and props up at the corner of the bar in a Dublin pub, surrounded by friends talking about everything and nothing. There is another sub-personality, an outsider, called Hank, who watches and observes. Hank is not a nice chap; he carries a knife (imaginary, of course) in a special holder in the small of his back, under his suit. Regardless of cost, Hank gets his way.

Problems occur when a sub-personality appropriate to one environment or time (e.g., childhood) shows up in a different context. Many years ago a director of a prestigious global investment bank told me a story about taking her daughter to see the headmistress of the daughter's school. They were asked to wait outside the headmistress's door on slightly uncomfortable metal frame seats, the sort you find in most educational institutions. The first sign that something was amiss was when she noticed a nervous sensation, butterflies in her tummy. The sense of nervousness increased as they were shown into the headmistress's office and directed to two equally uncomfortable seats in front of the headmistress's imposing desk, from behind which, in a rather more comfortable chair, the lady herself opened proceedings. My friend, for all her experience, status, and self-confidence, had unexpectedly reverted to her schoolgirl sub-personality.

You may have experienced something similar, say, as an adult visiting your parents' home and, on being asked to do the dishes, responding from a distinctly teenage place, an internal voice saying, "It's not my turn!" In my friend's case, she was quick enough and self-aware enough to manage the situation. She was, after all, paying the fees. Identifying and developing your sub-personalities and then making sure that the right one shows up is key to being successful. My Hank has his uses. I have not killed anyone or drawn blood, but sometimes hanging back from a situation, seeing what's going on, clarifying my intent, and then moving with focus and intensity can be a useful thing. Particularly when trying to getting on the Tube in London during rush hour—something I no longer do, for fear that Hank might reach for the knife.

What is being proposed in this section, multiple geniuses, is that your unique individual genius and your "sub-geniuses" will each have a somewhat different identity and will emphasize different elements of the "bundle". In truth, as Simon Williams. pointed out, there is not much difference between a unique individual genius and any "sub-genius". The purpose in making a distinction is to help in the development of genius by ensuring that in a world of limited time and resources, the chosen primary genius gets the required focus. But developing a second genius, or even more, might be beneficial. My career might require me to be a master of my craft while also demanding that I am a very competent leader, in which case I might look to develop my leadership genius. Or I may be approaching a change in my life such as a shift from full-time employment to self-employment. Beginning to develop skills or disciplines, a secondary marketing genius, say, before I make the shift might pay dividends. Or I may simply have a hobby or pastime, singing perhaps, that I would enjoy even more if my genius in it were expressed.

I have written in this chapter about the ideas of unique individual genius and multiple sub-geniuses framed within the much broader topic of identity. The purpose is to show that identity is not a fixed, immutable thing, but rather something that can be gently shaped in order that we as humans can thrive, be fulfilled, and express our innate genius(es).

CHAPTER FIVE

Mental State and Mindset

It is a beautiful sunny day in West London, Baron's Court to be precise, the home of The Queen's Club, an iconic British sports club. I am on a grass court hitting tennis balls with Tim Gallwey, author of the seminal Inner Game of Tennis. I am simply enjoying the day, enjoying hitting, enjoying being in Tim's company. Tim has other ideas. "Let's practise focusing," he suggests. So we do—he's the guru and I wasn't going to argue. He suggests a drill: each player suggests a quality that the other is to act out as we continue to hit balls. First he suggests, "Clumsy." I can't remember what I suggested for him. I try "clumsy" for a while, the only effect being to attract strange looks from the players on the next court. Tim suggests a variety of other qualities, which we play with, and then gives me "clown". I walk back to the baseline trying to act out "clown" and already it is not working. The image in my mind is the classic unruly red hair with male-pattern baldness, red nose, elbows every-where, and very big feet. As I pick up a ball I have to get a new image. This is of a different kind of clown, a really good one, with high energy and clear intent; with his attention projected into the watching crowd, unconscious of himself and his thoughts, not trying to be a clown, but clowning, alive. I take on the feelings around this second image and, acting out of it, put a ball into play. Within seconds I am lost in the game; totally present to the ball, to Tim, and the court; my attention externalized. The joy of playing takes over; my tennis playing is creative, *accurate, and fluent. I am "in the zone". In the zone I play my best ten-nis. Tim's intent in practising focusing, and doing these exercises was to generate a state of relaxed concentration and to move us both into flow.*

Mental state and mindset have a huge impact on the quality of any performance. Show up for any activity frustrated, distracted, and bored and the performance will be diminished and not much fun. Show up relaxed and focused and performance, learning, and joy are maximized. This is seen and experienced most easily in sports, the performing arts, and many martial arts. It can also be experienced in most other activities, as long as the activity is neither too boring nor too challenging. The point for us in the exploration of enabling genius is that the "right" mental state is key to excellence and thus key to enabling genius.

Before I go any further, I need to make a distinction between mental state and mindset. I think of these as being two different levels of function and use the terms "surface" and "deep". Mental state is surface; it is about the state of the mind, not the contents. It is whether one is "in the zone" or not, relaxed and focused, or stressed and distracted. It includes one's emotional state: joyful or fearful, for example. It is a minute-to-minute experience that can change swiftly. Mental state is like an interface between the mind and the experience.

Mindset is deep, more engrained; it is the contents of the mind, including beliefs, constructs, values, and attitudes. It prevails over periods of time but, critically, it can change. The one influences the other: if I don't trust my abilities, I am unlikely to find the zone. Or if I engage in an activity with a surface state of distraction and fear, I will certainly perform badly, perhaps fuelling a deeply held belief that I am not good at certain things.

Surface mental state requires the development of specific skills so that, for instance, you can be in the zone more deeply and more frequently or be able to regulate your emotional responses. Deep mindset requires an examination of one's beliefs, values, and attitudes. In the next few pages, we'll explore in greater detail surface-level mental state and deep-level mindset.

Mental State and the Impact on Performance

This mental state has been called many things; in the sporting world it is often called "being in the zone," as above. In psychology perhaps "flow", which was what its most famous student, Mihaly Csikszentmihalyi, called it. It is now the subject of much study, particularly by neurologists. Whatever you call it, it is essential to excellence and therefore to genius. My own understanding starts with the inner game. The book, *The Inner Game of Tennis,* was lying around the family house when I was in my early twenties and I read it through in one sitting. As I finished a page, a thought or a question would occur to me, which was then mysteriously taken up on the next page. For me it was an eye-opening occasion; many of the things that I struggled with as a player were explored there.

One of Gallwey's core models is:
Performance = Potential – Interference

Performance and potential you will understand. Interference is the new idea. It is anything that distracts you from putting your full attention on an activity—your thoughts, feelings, fears, doubts, hopes, questions, certainties, and uncertainties. What the model says is that if we can reduce the interference, our performance increases. There is a classic inner-game tennis exercise in which the student is asked to call out the word "bounce" when the ball hits the ground, and "hit" when it hits the strings of the racket. This is particularly successful with beginners because they have lots of interference going on, things like:

"I am useless at ball games."

"I am not coordinated."

"I hope I can hit it."

"I mustn't hit it into the net."

"What's a backhand?"

"Why is he laughing?"

"I really want to be good at this so that I can play with my family."

And more! All that stress, expectation, and distraction.

Calling "bounce" and "hit" has the effect of moving the attention away from the interference. As the student becomes absorbed in noticing the timing of the call in relation to the actual event and forgets about "doing it right" or getting the ball in, the mental state changes from fearful and distracted to that of relaxed concentration. Relaxed concentration is a term Gallwey used in place of "in the zone". In this mental state, performance increases. Better contact is made with the ball, the shots are more accurate, and the strokes more fluid. But that is not all, another thing happens that is even more astounding: the student learns without being taught. Let me give you an example. I will not presume that you know anything about tennis, but there is a different grip for each of the two basic strokes, forehand and backhand. When I was taught this, I was about thirteen at the time, it took me six months to get comfortable with the new grips. I have taken novices with absolutely no experience with tennis onto the court and taken them through the "bounce–hit" exercise. As they enter a state of relaxed concentration, the interference diminishes. As I throw a ball to the forehand and then to the backhand repeatedly, the student's hand begins to move on the handle toward the "correct" grips. What took me six months to get right is happening in minutes. I confess this always provokes amazement in me, even after 30 years, and an emotion that I can only describe as joy. It seems that when the mind is quiet and focused, the feedback that we pick up from our bodies and from the result of our actions conspire to enable fast, joyous learning. In flow we don't only perform to higher levels, we learn instinctively, just as we do as children—no one taught you how to walk, I am guessing. Our schooling makes us distrustful of ourselves, so that we look outside to others for teaching (rather than learning). Gallwey's model is useful, for it tells us that the first step in getting into flow is to remove or reduce any interference through focusing. On that sunny day at The Queen's Club we were not simply practising focusing, we were learning more about how to get into flow—and getting into flow is a skill, something we can get better at.

Flow and Mihaly Csikszentmihalyi

I have already made reference to Csikszentmihalyi and his work on flow. The state of "relaxed concentration", where there is minimal or no interference, is a flow state. In his book *Flow: The Psychology of Optimal Experience,* he has this to say:

"In the flow state, action follows upon action according to an internal logic that seems to need no conscious intervention by the actor."

Pete Sampras, American tennis player and winner of an amazing fourteen Grand Slams, was asked at the press conference after winning the 1999 Wimbledon final:

"What was on your mind when you served that winning ace?"
His response: *"There was absolutely nothing going through my mind."*

Clearly he was very skilled at getting into flow, for the pressure, the interference, was enormous. Daniel Goleman, who became famous as the author of *Emotional Intelligence*, makes the case for flow in his fabulous book, *Focus, the Hidden Driver of Excellence.* He has this to say:

Flow is a state of self-forgetfulness, the opposite of rumination and worry. People in flow exhibit a masterly control of what they are doing, their responses perfectly attuned to the changing demands of their task." And also: "People perform at their best in flow … the sheer pleasure of the act itself is what motivates them."

Csikszentmihalyi identified what he called the conditions of flow. He never, as far as I know, presented them as a list as I have done here, so what follows is my understanding:

- There are clear goals every step of the way.
- There is immediate feedback to one's actions.
- There is a balance between the challenges and the skills required.
- Action and awareness are merged.
- Distractions are excluded from consciousness.
- There is no worry of failure.
- Self-consciousness disappears.
- The activity becomes autotelic (from the Greek "auto", meaning self and "telos", goal. The idea is that simply engaging in the activity is its own reward. The achievement is in the doing).

Caroline Cryer gives us another insight in her article, "Models of Flow":

The release of neurochemicals in the brain contribute to the main stages of flow. In flow, the brain releases norepinephrine, dopamine, endorphins, anandamide, and serotonin. These five chemicals are the biggest rewards the brain can produce, and flow is one of the only times the brain produces all five simultaneously. First, adrenaline ensures we are alert and paying attention. Then norepinephrine is released, the hormone responsible for concentration. After this, dopamine is released, which enhances our pattern recognition; our brain starts telling us we're "on to something" in this phase, to keep paying attention, and to do more of it. These two chemicals combined help us ignore distractions while speeding up the connections between ideas. Then endorphins are released. These are the "happy" chemicals that help us feel invincible. Next, anandamide is released, which plays a role in helping us make connections, hence prompting lateral thinking. Finally, seratonin is released, the feel-good chemical. This combination of neurochemistry and brainwave states gives us access to solutions we don't normally have access to in normal consciousness, enabling us to make connections we wouldn't otherwise see.

Flow in the Workplace

In reading these descriptions, it may occur to you that flow only occurs in the realms of sports or the performing arts. But this is not so—all kinds of activities lend themselves to flow. Here are some examples:

- Thinking. I have a love/hate relationship with flying when traveling for business purposes. The hate bit is that it takes me away from home and my wife (and the dog, Delphine, a rescued Doberman. My stepdaughter has long left home). The love bit is that I frequently get into flow when traveling. I never watch the in-flight movies and I always have a notebook and a variety of pens at hand. At some point I'll get to thinking. There are few distractions, and thinking unfolds.
- Writing. Writing absolutely lends itself to flow—it's one of the reasons I do it. Plan well, make a mind-map of your thoughts, work out what you want your audience to think when they have read your piece, create a structure, set yourself a goal, close the door, turn off the phone and e-mail and write.
- Presentations. Rehearse your story until you know it backwards. Then, when live, focus on the audience.
- Meetings. Meetings that have a performance element, such as coaching sessions, sales meetings, or even facilitating meetings, can all be created as flow experiences.

Irena O'Brien, in her article, "The Science of Flow," writes:

One of the most comprehensive and detailed studies of how flow in the workplace contributes to optimal performance is that of Teresa Amabile and Steven Kramer (2011). They wanted to know what happens to people's thoughts, feelings, and motivations as they worked on solving complex problems … they found that, when people had a positive inner work life, they were more creative, more productive, and more committed to their work. They also found that progress in meaningful work, no matter how small, significantly influenced their inner work lives, leading to an upward spiral that they call the progress principle. This is important to companies because their bottom line depends on the performance of their people.

The Two Selves

Gallwey had a second way of thinking about flow, which provides us with a useful distinction; he called it the two selves or Self One and Self Two. As I understand it, Gallwey took a sabbatical during which time he taught tennis. One of the many things he noticed was that people playing tennis often had a very specific kind of conversation: a conversation with themselves. Those conversations, in my experience, usually follow an error. It begins with an expletive, followed by a criticism that is in turn followed by an instruction: *"****! (fill in your favourite) … your footwork stinks … keep your eye on the ball and stay on your toes."* Remember, this guy's playing for fun! Gallwey asked himself this question: "Who is talking to whom?" He answers his question thus:

Obviously, the who and the whom are separate entities or there would be no conversation, so that one could say that within each player there are two "selves". One seems to give instructions, the other seems to perform the action. Let's call the 'teller' Self One and the 'doer' Self Two.

I describe the two selves as follows (these are my words and not Gallwey's):

- Self One is the internalized voice of our parents, teachers, and those in authority. Self One seeks to control Self Two and does not trust it. Self One is characterized by fear and doubt, and by trying too hard.

- Self Two is the whole human being, with access to all its potential and capacities, including the hard-wired capability to learn. It is characterized by relaxed concentration, trust in oneself, and by the experience of joy.

I find the Self One – Self Two distinction very useful and practical, as do many others, as it is relatively easy to answer the question "Are you in Self One or Self Two?" And wearing an "enabling" hat, it is also relatively easy to observe when someone else is in one or the other of those states.

Self Two and flow are both descriptions of a mental state where high performance, learning, and joy occur: genius by another name.

To bring to a close this piece on mental state, I want to draw attention briefly to the relationship of deliberate practice, mentioned in chapter two, with flow. The effect of deliberate practice is to move an activity from conscious competence to unconscious competence. What this means is that the performer has effectively removed a possible interference—how to perform a complex task—from his or her immediate awareness. And with the interference removed, the quality of the performance increases.

Mindset and the Impact on Performance

Here we shift from the surface level mental state to deep level mindset. When Gallwey identified the Two Selves, he did so on the basis of his day-to-day experience as a coach and player. That was in 1974. As the papers written by my colleagues show, there is now a wealth of scientific evidence that supports his proposition. One scientist working in this area has a formulation that is very close to Gallwey's and takes it into deep-state territory, as she includes beliefs about oneself. I am referring to Carol Dweck, the Lewis and Eaton Professor of Psychology at Stanford University. In her book, *Mindset,* Dweck tells of her research over a period of 20 years that shows how "The view you adopt for yourself profoundly affects the way you lead your life."

Her formulation suggests that there are two specific mindsets with which one can wander through life: a fixed mindset and a growth mindset. As I understand it, a fixed mindset is wrapped around a core belief that your abilities are "carved in stone"; all you have is what you are born with and there is nothing you can do about it. This can manifest itself in two quite different ways. One is a need to continually prove oneself. High achievers often fall into this category; they were born with talent, not like everyone else, and need to continually demonstrate this for validation. Dweck has this to say: "If you have only a certain amount of intelligence, a certain personality, and a certain moral character—well then, you had better prove that you have a healthy dose of them. It certainly wouldn't do to look deficient in these most basic characteristics." Dweck cites John McEnroe in this regard, he of the tantrums (in his tennis-playing days), and suggests that the tantrums were an expression of a fixed mindset: being so good that the ball simply could not have been out of bounds, the linesman or umpire must have made a mistake! The second way a fixed mindset operates is perhaps the more obvious: "I am no good, not naturally gifted, so I won't even try. I am the way I am!" In a fixed mindset, there is no opening for learning.

"The growth mindset is based on the belief that your basic qualities are things you can cultivate through your efforts," Dweck says. Someone with a growth mindset understands that achievement comes from developing your inherited gift, continually learning, and from persistence.

I cannot leave out the following, although it is a slight distraction from the story I am telling. Dweck draws attention to the work of Claude Steele of Stanford University and Joshua Aronson of the University of Texas. They performed an experiment in which a group of people of mixed race, gender, and age were given a test.

They were then given a second test of similar difficulty, but this time they were required to indicate their racial heritage, gender, and age. Most people's scores fell but older, black women's scores fell by far the most significantly!

In bringing these factors into awareness, interference, to use Gallwey's term, was generated—the idea that I might be less capable because of my gender, age, or racial background. This effect has become known as the stereotype threat. It strongly suggests that culturally shared stereotypes disrupt performance. A kind of collective interference, if you like.

Sue Coyne and James Gairdner, in their article on mindset, go further into the "content" of what I have called the "deep level":

Mindset is: the neural blueprint that creates our view of the world and our way of being in the world. Mindset is multi-layered. They describe these layers as:

- *Identity—Who am I?*
- *Purpose—Why am I here?*
- *Values*
- *Attitudes and Beliefs*
- *Talent/Gifts*
- *Intention (stance)*
- *Behaviours/skills/capabilities*
- *Experiences*

Simply, a genius mindset occurs when there is complete alignment between (the layers of) mindset. A state where there is no dissonance between layers and which creates the possibility for genius to flow. It is our contention that just as 'interference' adversely impacts the ability of individuals to express their full potential, so dissonance between layers interrupts the flow of genius and the expression of genius in our context. So:

Expression = Genius − Dissonance.

This last sentence reflects Gallwey's model on potential shown earlier.

In this chapter we have focused on and revealed the territory of surface-level mental state and deep-level mindset and positioned them both as being critical to excellence and thus critical to genius. A number of my colleagues believe that flow is perhaps the most important component in enabling genius, and I can't disagree. Being in flow is also a source of great joy. Later in this book we will come back to flow, mental state, and mindset and discuss how to get into flow.

CHAPTER SIX

Desire

If one thinks about high achievers from any walk of life, thoughts may turn to the rewards for their performance and then, maybe, to what drives them not just to achieve, but also to work toward their goals and to persist over time. Drive or motivation is obviously a key ingredient in success, particularly long-term success such as over a career; these are clearly a "pillar". However, I think many of us relate to drive as something one is either blessed with or not, that we have or do not have. In the context of this book on enabling genius, this way of thinking demands some examination because if we are born with a fixed quotient of will, then I would never have made it past my teenage years, when I found it difficult to even contemplate getting out of bed, let alone doing anything useful with my life. To set out on a path toward genius requires many things, among them a strong, persistent desire and, for most of us, we will need to develop it.

Earlier in the book I offered a partial explanation about why I am calling this pillar "desire". I hope that by the end of the chapter the reasons will be transparently clear. Motivation and drive, and even will, are all words that I have used in the past to describe this pillar and in many ways they all will do, but they don't nail it. I want to get to something that is more useful in the context of enabling genius. For genius, in its infancy, is a delicate thing requiring subtle attention and gentleness more than the raw horsepower of an unbridled will. The nature of many things so far discussed here is that they are emergent and change over time. They are in fact always in the process of development and, as such, like anything small and growing, require care and attention. Not being open to how one's genius is evolving and, say, sticking with goals identified in another time—in another moment of understanding—and perhaps even identified by someone else (a parent, teacher, manager, or coach) is a recipe for frustration, heartache and, ultimately, failure. In choosing the word desire, and defining it as I do here, the intention is to bring a more intentional yet forgiving energy to motivation, an energy that is more about emerging purpose than rigid goals and that can embrace mistakes and changes of mind without invalidating itself.

Intrinsic and Extrinsic Motivation

As with many things in this book, even a cursory glimpse at the literature on motivation and related topics will reveal a vast and complicated world. In order to get a useful grip on the topic, some simplification is required. In this spirit let me suggest that, in the area of motivation, three principle drives can be identified from the literature. The first of these is the most basic: the drive to survive. This embraces the need to find food and water, for sex and affection (without love the human being, as a baby specifically, dies). The source of this drive is internal.

The second is perhaps less basic, but no less fundamental: the drive to fit in. A part of the success story of the human race is the capacity to cooperate with each other, initially for the purpose of defence, and later to be more efficient hunter-gatherers. Not only were specific behaviours and skills required for these activities, such as the dividing of responsibilities, but also certain values were required to allow small groups of people to get along together, such as respect for another's property. The source of this second drive is external—the rewards and punishment meted out by one's fellow humans.

For a long time it was thought that everything could be reduced to these two drives, until something happened that at the time was seen as extraordinary. Professor Harry Harlow of the University of Wisconsin performed an experiment about learning using monkeys, in which the monkeys acted in a very specific way without being subjected to any external stimulus or driven by the need for food or sex. The center of the experiment was a puzzle in which the monkey had to undo a hinged flap that had been secured with a number of pins. Harlow put the puzzle into the cage prior to the experiment so that the monkeys would get familiar with it. However, and to his surprise, driven simply by curiosity and playfulness, the monkeys started to solve the problem before the experiment had begun. A third drive had been identified and it was labelled "intrinsic motivation", for there was no reward for the behaviours other then the actual doing of it. To quote Harlow: *"The performance of the task provided intrinsic reward."*

The publication of the results created such a backlash from those invested in the then-current thinking—which was more identified with the two more basic drives mentioned earlier—that Harlow set aside his work and went on to other things. Harlow was doing this work in the late 1940s and it was not until Edward Deci came along some 20 years later that the cause was taken up again with full vigour. Deci was then a graduate psychology student at Carnegie Mellon University in Pittsburgh and had a deep interest in motivation.

Beyond Carrot-and-Stick

An early experiment he conducted with some students produced results that built on Harlow's thesis. He divided the students into two groups and ran three sessions in which the students were given problems to solve. The first group was not rewarded in session one, but was rewarded in session two (the price of a couple of beers), and in the third session went unrewarded again. The second group was never rewarded. During each session, Deci left the room for a short period and went into an adjoining room from where he could observe the students. Here's what he saw:

Session 1: Both groups spent a few minutes of the time Deci was absent continuing to work on the puzzle.

Session 2: Having been paid, the first group spent about 50% more time in which Deci was absent on the puzzle. The second group, still unpaid, spent about the same amount of time as they did in session one (a few minutes).

Session 3: Both groups were unpaid. The first group, now unpaid, spent less time when he was absent than they had in the *first* session. The second group, still unpaid, actually spent a little more time than the first session.

If the experiment had been stopped after the second session, popular belief about motivation would have been confirmed. After all, that is how lots of parents convince their children to do homework or study for an exam—promise a reward. But the experiment did not stop there. It was of course the third session that was surprising, though not to Deci; he probably would not have set the experiment up if he was expecting a different kind of result. Rewarding the first group eroded any enjoyment inherent to the task, so that by the third session they hardly engaged at all during the break. The second group, which had not had their enjoyment spoiled, stayed engaged. Deci said this: "When money is used as an external reward for some activity, the subjects lose intrinsic interest in the activity."

I should also point out that intrinsic motivation has a strong connection with flow; one of Csikszentmihalyi conditions being that the activity becomes autotelic as described in the previous chapter.

"Intrinsic motivation exists within the individual and lies in either the enjoyment or interest in the task itself—or both, for interest and enjoyment are different. The reward is in the doing of it rather than an external pressure, punishment or reward."

This is what Daniel Pink, well-known author of many business books, wrote in a great book on motivation: *Drive—the Surprising Truth about What Motivates Us.*

Extrinsic motivation derives from forces outside of the individual, such as rewards, pressure, and punishment. The effects tend to be short lived and intrinsic motivation is eroded. To be clear, it is not that extrinsic motivation always has negative consequences; there are some situations where it works well, for instance, routine tasks that do not involve a need for much thinking or focus, particularly if the tasks are to be completed in the short term. Equally, an extrinsic reward for completing a task or achieving an objective can add to the overall motivation. It is the sole reliance on extrinsic motivation that has negative consequences. I think of all the "prodigies" pushed on by parents and coaches, who, when they reach the age of majority—either legally or in a psychological sense—and they assume some control of themselves, their actions, and decisions, they tend to give up the pursuit they once apparently loved. Or simply burned out.

Extrinsic motivation plays a huge role in the way many if not most businesses are led and managed; "carrot and stick" is the underlying principle in most approaches to performance management. The very words "performance management" suggest a way of thinking about human beings that might be more appropriate to getting a higher milk yield from a herd of cattle. "Talent management" is no better. And as for "human resources", well, I guess you could milk them too!

That the effect of extrinsic motivation is counterproductive is beyond question and yet many business organizations employ it almost exclusively. Given that no behaviour is accidental, "management" must be getting something, some valued outcome from sticking with an approach that not only doesn't work, but has negative consequences. As a marker of the negative consequences, Gallup's 2014 survey of the US workforce indicates that 31.5% are engaged in their work, 51% are not engaged, and 17.5% are actively disengaged. As to what management gets from this, two things come to mind. The first is that one is unlikely to be criticized for doing something the way it has always been done and, secondly, an approach based on extrinsic motivation gives management the illusion of being in control. And the price of the illusion is horrific.

Love and Will

In chapter four, when talking about identity, I mentioned Roberto Assagioli, the "father" of psychosynthesis. He had a useful way of looking at motivation that he describes in his book, *The Act of Will.* Will is almost an old-fashioned word not much in use today. It carries with it a Victorian sense of self-denial, self-sacrifice, and coldness, values not appreciated in our buy-now-pay-later, "entitled" culture. Assagioli sheds light on a critical aspect of desire and motivation: the interplay and ultimately the synthesis of love and will. Assagioli identified love and will as two fundamental human attributes. Will is the capacity to have desires and to act intentionally toward achieving them. In philosophical terms, it is important as it is seen as a distinct part of one's mind, alongside other attributes such as reason and understanding. In psychological terms, will is seen as a fundamental function. Assagioli says this in *The Act of Will:*

Fundamental to (man's) inner powers, and the one to which priority should be given, is the tremendous, unrealized potential of man's own will. There are two reasons for this: the first is the will's central position in man's personality and its intimate connection with the core of his being—his very self. The second lies in the will's function in deciding what is to be done, in applying all the necessary means for its realization, and in persisting in the task in the face of all obstacles and difficulties.

Love is so many things to so many people that I am not going to risk a definition—or write a poem, which, other than songs, seems to be the most common route to understanding and communicating about love. Not something for this book! However, it is accurate to suggest that love's fundamental function is to bring people together for a variety of purposes: procreation, nurturing, and acting together for the common good, either to protect against threats or to achieve a collective aim such as growing a crop or capturing a beast for food. So it is an aspect of the two basic drives mentioned earlier: to survive and to fit in.

Assagioli suggests that love and will exist in a kind of inverse proportionality, that a person with strong will has a lesser capacity for love and a person with a strong capacity for love is weaker in the will department.

He also presented them as two opposing poles:

- Will is a more "masculine" energy and love more "feminine".
- Will is "head", the rational intellectual, while love is "heart", or intuitive.
- Will seeks control; love trusts and lets things happen.
- Will looks for structure; love for process.

The Synthesis of Love and Will

Both love and will have positive and negative aspects. Love is part of nurturing one's offspring. So is will, in providing boundaries within which the child can explore. These are clearly positive. But they also have negative aspects; an overly nurturing parent may be too protective and not allow the child to take risks or learn from the consequences of his or her actions. Similarly, an overly controlling parent, teacher, or manager may well rob the child, student, or staff member of the opportunity to exercise their intrinsic motivation or to take responsibility. These two examples are about love and will, and they show up in our relationships with others. They also show up in how we relate to ourselves, in this case in relation to motivation. Will clearly has a positive aspect in decision-making and persistence. It is tempered by love, or "love of self", as Assagioli called it, in say, taking care of oneself by not pushing beyond one's limits.

According to Assagioli, the first job is to balance these capacities. If will is stronger than the love attribute, then love should be developed and strengthened, and vice versa. The second is to move beyond the polarity. As Assagioli wrote:

The essential requirement ... is to avoid identifying with either of the poles, and to control, transmute, and direct their energies from a higher unifying center of awareness and power.

This is not about making a simple compromise. It is to synthesize the best of both within the individual and to seek an authentic and congruent modality. One of the rules of such a synthesis is "to transcend and include". Let me explain that a bit more. It kind of follows from something that Einstein said: "A problem is never resolved at the level of consciousness at which it was created." 'Transcend' means to move up a level—in this case, of consciousness and awareness. "Include", in this context, means that both poles are present in the form of the best of both attributes.

I met my stepdaughter, Vicky, when she was four years old. At the time of writing she is a young woman of thirty-one. In the early days, it took me a long while to work out how to be a stepfather. I was genuinely confused as to what my "rights" were. One early attempt at suggesting that something should be done differently drew the response, "You're not my daddy!" Fair enough! That put me in my place and I allowed it to delay the process of my becoming a responsible parent and establishing the boundaries that would allow Vicky to be safe and to develop. Eventually it became clear to me, with the help of a very good psychotherapist, that not only did I have rights, I also had responsibilities. But that was only the beginning of the process. I come from an Irish Catholic family of six children; Vicky and my wife, Jo, are both from single-child families. The rules are not the same from one family type to the other and I noticed that I was seeking to impose the rules that I had learned in my larger Irish context. I needed to rise above the situation, balance my desire for control with the intent to nurture, and help create an agreement that allowed us all to function as a family. And we did, mostly. There was an unexpected and delightful consequence to this. As any fool knows—except this one it seems—bottling up "stuff" doesn't work. In my holding back from setting boundaries and seeing Vicky conduct herself in ways that I thought inappropriate (occasionally, I hasten to add), I would get irritated, but not say anything. That kind of irritation cannot not be communicated, no matter how hard you try. When we made our agreements, a lot of rubbish and interference were removed from the relationship and there was more room for love.

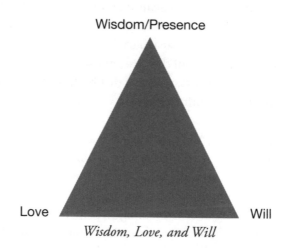

Wisdom, Love, and Will

"Wisdom" and "presence" are two words that Assagioli used to represent this synthesis of love and will. As I understand this—that's to say this is not what I have read directly in the works of Assagioli—love and will show up differently depending on the context. In the context of my relationship with others, as a parent, teacher, or manager, for instance, love and will are outwardly directed and presence, the non-judgmental, listening attitude, is most helpful. In the context of managing myself, inwardly directed, the representation of the synthesis might be "wisdom". That said, this next proposition is mine and not part of the psychosynthesis cannon. I am suggesting that the word "desire" is a candidate for the synthesis of love and will in the context of motivation.

Desire

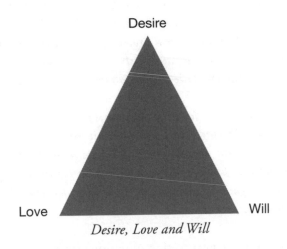

Desire, Love and Will

Desire can be used to mean a fleeting pang or urge, perhaps something trivial that requires satiation. Or in matters of the heart, as in the "object of my desire," it may refer to a romantic or sexual drive. True desire, I hold, is congruent with one's sense of identity: one's sense of self and sense of purpose. It embraces the best of will and the best of love. It is persistent and endures over time, and it flexes in the face of changes in circumstance. It is a primary source of energy. Desire emerges from within; it is primarily an intrinsic motivation. True desire fuels and sustains genius.

Ian Harrison relates this anecdote concerning his daughter, Ruth:

At 16, Ruth had reached grade seven piano and grade five violin. Her heart was set on pursuing a career as a musician and her intention was to apply to attend a conservatoire after her a-levels were complete. She had taken a significant step toward her dream by winning a place in a junior conservatoire to study for her grade eight exam. That year proved valuable in unexpected ways. The expectation and discipline of the junior conservatoire brought clarity about what was required to achieve her dream. It also brought clarity about what she really wanted from her musical talent—and it wasn't to be a professional musician.

In the context of "motivation", Ruth lost her motivation. In the context of "drive", she lost her drive. In the context of "desire", she understood that she didn't really want to be a professional musician. At the end of her year in the junior conservatoire, she passed her grade eight piano exam and left the conservatoire to focus on her other studies.

Now pursuing her passion for literature, she is studying for her degree in English literature. During her first year at university, Ruth has saved up to restore an old violin she was given and plays both piano and violin with great pleasure. Junior conservatoire was an invaluable experience for her because it gave her a chance to explore her desires and to understand where music fits into her life.

Before moving to the next section, one thing strikes me powerfully that I want to mention. You have a will. It is both part of you and apart from you. You can influence your will—recognising this is the first step. Some while back I strained my hamstring while running. The physiotherapist gave me some treatment and exercises to complete, but told me I should not run for a few weeks. Seeing my disappointment, she said that after a few days I could start walking and that an hour would be about right. The first time I went out for my walk I got very bored and decided to take a shortcut home. At that very moment something caused me to pause and the voice in my head asked: "What does your will want?" Up until that moment the lazy part of me had been the only voice; now I was hearing that there was another element in play, my will, and that I had a choice in the matter. So I asked my will what it wanted and it wanted to walk and complete the hour, which is what I did. The second step is to know that you can develop your will so it is more powerful, and this is clearly important in enabling genius, where the obstacles are numerous. Assagioli suggests that simple exercises can help in this regard, such as deciding to do something and sticking with it. In the beginning this might be quite trivial, such as reading a chapter of a book every day.

Autonomy, Mastery, and Purpose

For the purposes of understanding genius and what it takes to enable it, I want to draw attention to a central part of Daniel Pink's work on motivation, as described in *Drive*. According to him, there are three fundamental elements: autonomy, mastery, and purpose. He seems to have missed that this makes "amp" (ampere), a unit of electrical current, which seems appropriate.

Autonomy

Autonomy is "the power or right to self-govern" according to the *Chamber's English Dictionary*. Pink tells us that Edward Deci, mentioned earlier, teamed up with Richard Ryan, now professor of psychology, psychiatry, and education at the University of Rochester, New York, and between them they contributed enormously to the understanding of motivation and what it is. One such contribution is self-determination theory (SDT). Pink says this:

STD ... begins with a notion of universal human needs. It argues that we have three innate psychological needs: competence, autonomy, and relatedness. When those needs are satisfied, we're motivated, productive, and happy.

And this:

According to a cluster of recent Behavioural science studies, autonomous motivation promotes greater conceptual understanding, better grades, enhanced persistence at school and in sporting activities, higher productivity, less burnout, and greater levels of psychological wellbeing.

Let's do more of that then!

And then this:

"We are born to be players, not pawns."

In this last quote, the suggestion is that we are born free, with a desire for autonomy (in the psychological sense, not the physical sense, for as babies we are dependent on our parents) and that this is smothered. Smothered by the habits and practices of our communities trying to turn us into good citizens—a negative impact of extrinsic motivation and the drive to fit in.

Pink goes on to explain that there are four areas in particular in which people require autonomy:

- Autonomy of task: I get to choose, to a significant degree, what I do.
- Autonomy of time: I get to choose when I do it.
- Autonomy of technique: I get to choose how I do it.
- Autonomy of team: I get to choose, or a least have a vote in, whom I work with.

I use the word "authority" as a synonym of autonomy. Authority has the same Latin root as the word "author"; a writer, someone who creates. That root is "auctum", which means to produce, increase, or cause to grow. An author writes his own book. An editor dictating the structure and words of the book would soon wear the patience of the writer, turning him into a mere scribe and undermining his authority. Any erosion of authority, of autonomy, destroys the will. Anything that develops authority feeds and enhances the will, desire. A health degree of authority and autonomy is fundamental to enabling genius.

Mastery

A master is one who commands or controls. Mastery is, according to *Chambers,* "supreme skill or knowledge" that gives the master the kind of control that enables great works. If an individual does not have the required skills to achieve their goals they will lose interest, which in turn will undermine their will. Conversely, if an individual does have the required skills and begins to see some success, then motivation is enhanced.

Richard Sennett, in his book *The Craftsman,* points to the intrinsic motivation that comes from mastery when he writes: *"Craftsmanship names an enduring, basic human impulse: the desire to do a job well for its own sake."*

This notion clearly finds reflection in that of deliberate practice, for mastery cannot be achieved without practice. It finds further confirmation in Csikszentmihalyi's conditions for flow: that the activity is autotelic, the reward is inherent in the execution of the task or skill.

Purpose

The *Chamber's English Dictionary* comes to my aid again; purpose is *"an idea or aim kept in mind as a goal toward which one's efforts are directed."* Pink uses the word in a slightly different way. He writes of having a sense of purpose in the way that I would talk about work having meaning. And this in turn builds motivation and feeds desire. Pink writes:

The most deeply motivated people—not to mention those who are the most productive and satisfied—hitch their desires to a cause larger than their own.

As this chapter comes to a close, I want to bring the thinking back to enabling genius and its relationship to desire. Pink, in *Drive*, writes:

They (scientists from institutions across the world) have produced hundreds of research papers, most of which point to the same conclusion. Human beings have an innate drive to be autonomous, self-determined, and connected to one another. And when that drive is liberated, people achieve more and live richer lives.

True desire, as I am defining it here, embraces intrinsic and extrinsic motivation, where the latter has a positive impact. It also embraces autonomy, authority, purpose and mastery, meaning and connectedness. Without the energy of desire, nothing happens, certainly not genius. Moreover, it is the fuel of genius. And it can be developed.

CHAPTER SEVEN

Learning

There is no genius without learning. No one gets put on the planet as a fully developed, de facto genius, the finished article. Or anything close. Genius requires development, and conscious, intentional learning is the key. In the Pillars of Genius model, learning is shown at the center because it impacts all the other pillars: identity, mindset, mental state, and desire. This reflects a major theme in this book; namely, that almost all our attributes as human beings can be developed.

It is central to this story of enabling genius and it is, in a sense, where the story started with Ericson's research and the discovery of the ten-year rule and the idea of deliberate practice.

Learning as the Key to Genius

Gallwey tells a frightening story about working with a fast-moving consumer goods manufacturer, a globally recognized brand, which asked him to address the top few hundred people in the organization. At the mid-point break in his presentation, his host asked him not to use the "L word". Gallwey racked his brain but could not identify an expletive beginning with "L". Seeing his confusion, his host clarified: "Learning. These guys have arrived—they don't need to learn!" You can imagine the amazement. Later Gallwey got to speak with the president of the company and told him this story. The president took it in, thought a bit, and declared: "They must learn!" Not himself—they! He then appointed a vice president of learning and that was the end of it. Since that day I have asked many of the senior people that I coach what they are focused on learning, only to be met with an uncomprehending, blank look. It is utterly confounding to me that learning is held in such low regard in many societies. People talk about education in political or academic circles without actually talking about learning. I can understand why this has come about—hours spent in classrooms, distraction from play, learning meaningless stuff by rote, the quality of much teaching, and exams. Not much joy there!

Sir Anthony Seldon, former master at Wellington College in England and a well-known political author, in a paper entitled, "An End to Factory Schools," published by the Center for Policy Studies in 2010, opens with these words:

Schools should be places of engagement and delight. Instead, students often resent and insufficiently value them. Parents should be actively engaged in and full of gratitude for the schools that their children attend. Instead, they are often indifferent and even uncooperative. Teaching should be a profession that the brightest and most energetic should aspire to and fight to join. Instead, it is hard to get top graduates to apply. And when they do, it is hard to keep them in the profession (which is a profession in name alone). To be a school head should be the apex of every teacher's dream. Instead, such is the encumbered nature of the job, many head posts remain unfilled.

Harsh words, but as a teacher and headmaster he should know. I am nonetheless surprised that so little is done to change this. If the joy of learning was revealed to children or, more accurately, not beaten out of them, so very much would change. Recently, after a tennis lesson, a mother who was watching her son on the next court caught my eye and said, "I have never seen anyone enjoying tennis so much. It's a pleasure to see." Now, I was a little hacked off at first because what I really wanted her to say was that my backhand was amazing. But a second's reflection had me realize that this was the best feedback anybody could ever give me. A part of the pleasure in playing is the simple satisfaction of performing. And at least an equal part is the joy of learning, and I had not anticipated that. As we know, all the "gifted" and "naturals" in any discipline have spent hour upon hour learning and practicing: a new challenge is greeted with pleasure and to meet it one must learn, change, and adapt.

Roger Federer, acknowledged by many as one of the greatest, if not the best tennis player of all time, is an extraordinary and inspiring example of embracing learning. He lost in the semi-finals of the 2011 US Open to Novak Djokovic (another great exemplar of learning), a match he had been on the point of winning. At 30 years of age, no one would have said a word if he had hung up his rackets and retired. What he did was to go away for a few weeks and develop certain aspects of his game. He came back and had an extraordinary streak of wins. The year 2013 was a bad one for Federer, as he struggled with illness and injury; the pundits were writing him off. News leaked out that he had tried a new racket just before that year's US Open—he lost in the fourth round, his earliest exit in years. Through the "off season", he worked with his new racket, and added more power, more reach, and more spin and in the new season duly reclaimed his place among the top three in the game. But he did not stop there. He hired a new coach, Stefan Edberg, a Swede and former champion, one of the best serve and volley exponents. This allowed him to develop a new attacking edge to his game. At the time of writing we have just seen him beat Scotland's Andy Murray (who played brilliantly!) in straight sets in the Wimbledon semi-finals. This was quite possibly the best tennis played by one man—ever. He could not quite recapture that form in the final, losing to Djokovic. This is a story of learning, a story of genius.

It's a Process

In reading David Shenk's *The Genius in All of Us*, I was struck by a line he used in a story he told about an American baseball player of great fame (apparently; baseball is a mystery to me). Ted Williams played for the Boston Red Sox from 1939–1960 with a four-year interruption during the war. He was held in almost God-like esteem, his skills described as exquisite and, yes, he was seen as being "innately gifted". He knew differently, however, and said as much; "It was a load of bull, Nothing except practise, practise, and practise will bring out that ability."

Williams would practise as a kid in the local park, hitting balls until they fell apart. He used what little pocket money he had to bribe his friends to play with him. You get the picture. Here is what Shenk had to say about this, the line that stood out:

"Greatness was not a thing to Ted Williams; it was a process."

A few pages later he takes the idea up again, almost as a refrain:

"Talent is not a thing; it's a process."

It's a process: something that moves from one state or stage to another. The output is consolidation; the outcome is excellence. Deliberate practice is a part of the process of enabling genius.

Irena O'Brien found this quote from Mary Oliver, the American Pulitzer-Prize-winning poet: *"How many roads did St. Augustine go down before he became St. Augustine?"*

Sugar Man

There is an American musician, Rodriguez, of whom you may have heard. He produced two albums in the 1970s that did not sell particularly well and he pretty much disappeared. The rumour was that he had died. However, his music slowly developed a cult-like following in Australia, New Zealand, and South Africa. A wonderful film, *Searching for Sugarman* (Sugarman is the name of one of his songs), tells the story of how two men linked up to find out more about him and discovered him alive and well in Detroit. With their help, he went back to performing and is currently touring to great acclaim. In between the release of his two albums and his rediscovery, Rodriquez married, had a family, became interested in local politics, and worked without complaint for a construction firm. In the film, the owner of that firm, who had known nothing of Rodriquez's musical past but clearly held him in high regard, is interviewed and said this: "He keeps on refining the process of how he applies himself." Learning. Genius.

Deliberate Practice

Deliberate practice is a planned approach to a highly intentional practice designed to improve specific skills to expert levels. The task or exercise is constantly repeated, with the subject receiving immediate, specific, and relevant feedback. Ericsson and his colleagues wrote about the origin of deliberate practice in their report, "The Role of Deliberate Practice in the Acquisition of Expert Performance." The teachers they refer to initially, music teachers, and the individual instruction they provided, rather than group lessons, was seen to be the best path to expert performance.

Given the cost of individualized instruction, the teacher designs practice activities that the individual can engage in between meetings with the teacher. We call these practice activities 'deliberate practice' and distinguish them from other activities, such as playful interaction, paid work, and observation of others, that individuals can pursue in the domain.

And in the same report they write:

On the basis of several thousand years of education, along with more recent laboratory research on learning and skill acquisition, a number of conditions for optimal learning and improvement of performance have been uncovered (Bower and Hilgard, 1981; Gagne, 1970). The most-cited condition concerns the subjects' motivation to attend to the task and exert effort to improve their performance. In addition, the design of the task should take into account the pre-existing knowledge of the learners so that the task can be correctly understood after a brief period of instruction. The subjects should receive immediate informative feedback and knowledge of the results of their performance. The subjects should repeatedly perform the same or similar tasks. When these conditions are met, practice improves accuracy and speed of performance on cognitive, perceptual, and motor tasks.

You might have noticed the reference to motivation, which is a nice link to the previous chapter, "Desire".

In my personal genius project to return to playing competitive tennis, Craig and I started with identifying what my unique genius as a tennis player might be. Having this straight (and I am not writing it here as I do not want to give any possible opponent an insight), we got clear about what that looks like in play. We then examined my technique and approach to playing to see where the shortfalls were—and the strengths. As a function of these two inputs—the intended way of playing and my strengths and weaknesses—we began to design my deliberate practice. Some of the practice happens under Craig's watchful eye and some with paid "hitters" (good juniors or players on their way to becoming coaches). The hitters were initially surprised to see me turn up with a plan for the session, one remarking, "You really are intense, aren't you?" Here is an example of the deliberate practice we designed for a relatively simple technique I had to learn. I wrote earlier that we had to change every stroke in my repertoire. In my case, that meant significant changes in the way I hold the racket for both my forehand and backhand. The deliberate practice sequence was this:

1. Craig hand-feeds balls to my forehand until I get comfortable with the grip. Repeat for the backhand.
2. Craig racket-feeds balls to my forehand until I am comfortable with the increase in pace. Repeat for backhand.
3. Craig hand-feeds ball alternately to my forehand and backhand until I get comfortable changing grips.

You get the picture. Some months and many steps later I am working with a hitter:

4. Rallying with the hitter. Hitter hits a sequence of three balls to my forehand, which I have to return cross-court. He hits the fourth ball to my backhand, which I have to return down the line. Start again.

It's exhausting. But with deliberate practice and a gradual ramping up of the difficulty, both my performance and confidence are improving.

Deliberate Practice in Work

As I have observed before, sports and the performing arts are wonderful laboratories for experimentation and observation and provide great examples to help explain some of the principles at work. The results are immediate and measureable, so any change in behaviours, mindset, or mental state can be, to some degree, observed and measured. Deliberate practice does happen in work, I suggest, just not frequently enough or with sufficient awareness and intent. As an example, most training programmes have an element of deliberate practice: something new is introduced, and if it is a skill it might be demonstrated and the participants practise it. Meetings, sales meetings, sales calls, and presentations all lend themselves to some form of deliberate practice. Aristotle Onassis, the Greek shipping magnate, famous for his great wealth, his relationship with Maria Callas and later his marriage to Jacqueline Kennedy, the former wife of American President John F. Kennedy (did you really need to know all that? Anyway, that Onassis), practised meetings with his team (the rest of us just complain about them). Role-play, rehearsal, and visualization are all potential means of deliberate practice.

Permit me a small diversion—meetings. People do complain about them. Meetings are a critical tool to leverage performance—or a waste of time. To those who complain: either don't go or get good at them!

Back to enabling genius. I had a telephone call a few weeks ago with an old friend, an architect, and mentioned the enabling genius project. He asked about the relevance for him. The conversation went a bit like this:

Me	*So what are you great at, as an architect?*
Him	*Understanding the client, their needs and aims, and creating the brief.*
Me	*And what are you less good at?*
Him	*The creative problem-solving.*
Me	*Which of those two is most interesting to get better at?*
Him	*The second.*
Me	*How could you practise that?*
Him	*I could find an old brief and create three new solutions for it.*

Clearly there were many "Ums" and "I don't knows" in the conversation.

Some activities are so singular and the variables so numerous that setting up practice is next to impossible. And fitting in 10,000 hours of practice may prove difficult, so the alternative is to indulge in a little real-time practice. This can be done by identifying an element of your work skill set that you want to develop and then using real work-based opportunities to practice. Federer is known to do this; when he is comfortably in control of a match, he will often try out new tactics or a shot or stroke that he is working on. The quality of such practice can be enhanced greatly with planning, awareness in action, and review—there's more on this later in this chapter under the heading "Designing Learning and Deliberate Practice."

Deliberate Practice and Flow

Here are some of the critical variables involved in deliberate practice:

- The quantity (number of repetitions) involved in the practice
- The quality of the practice; the intensity and focus the subject brings to the activity
- The motivation of the subject; the quality of the design of the practice; the quality of the feedback from the teacher or coach.

There is another variable for which I can only find one relevant research paper and it is this: whether the subject is in flow or not—whether they are in Gallwey's Self Two or stuck in Self One. The research paper is by McKay, B., Wulf, G., Lewthwaite, R., and Nordin, A. (2015) and is entitled, "The Self: Your own Worst Enemy?" about a test of the self-invoking trigger hypothesis, published in *The Quarterly Journal of Experimental Psychology*. In a series of three tests, the subjects were required to throw darts at a target. Between throwing the darts, one sub-group was given tasks that required self-reflection while the second, a control group, was not. What they found is that any self-focus, rather than an external focus, is detrimental to performance. This would seem to suggest that deliberate practice in flow will be optimally effective, but there is clearly more research required.

In the chapter on mental state and mindset I told of my experience as an inner game coach, during which I noticed that people learned quite complex techniques without being taught. My job as the coach was less about teaching and more about helping my clients get into a Self-Two state, or flow, because I knew that once there, in flow, they would learn, accessing the self-same innate learning mechanism that they used to learn to walk and talk. Society and schooling may have ignored this, but the capacity did not go away, it still resides in us no matter how neglected. Deliberate practice in a state of flow, I argue, will significantly increase the quality of the practice and, again I argue, will reduce the amount of time required to achieve expert levels of performance. The other side of this is that with increased practice in getting into flow, the performer will be more able to get into flow when performing and potentially be able to bring that skill to other tasks.

Deliberate practice that is not designed with flow in mind will still have the effect of easing the subject into that state when performing. As part of my genius tennis project, Craig and I identified specific sequences of strokes that I practise regularly. These sequences are consistent with and are a function of my unique, individual tennis genius. Let me illustrate this with an example. I am left-handed. When I hit a forehand cross-court, which is the most natural direction, it goes to my opponent's backhand, usually the weakest stroke. The deliberate practice sequence is to hit two balls cross-court, the second pulling the opponent off court, and then hit one down the line into the vacated space. Point over! There was an unexpected consequence of this: in certain situations when I am playing, I no longer have to think about where to hit the next ball, the decision is already made, and thus interference is reduced (performance = potential – interference). And I am much more likely to get into flow.

Learning

There is a distinction to be made between deliberate practice and learning, and it is this: learning is the acquisition of new skills, behaviours, and knowledge and the development of them; getting better at what you have already learned. The role of practice is to consolidate the learning: to move from conscious incompetence to conscious competence. Clearly one learns during practice, but the purpose of each activity is different. This is why in my tennis project I work with my coach, Craig, to learn and develop a specific aspect of my game and then practise with others to consolidate and create new habits.

In reading and researching for this book, I got swallowed up by a universe of competing educational theories. The job here is to simplify and remain pragmatic, to understand what's going to help in enabling genius. The piece that most requires highlighting is another key distinction: learning that comes from within an individual and learning that comes from without. Learning that comes from without is mostly called teaching. Learning that comes from within is sometimes called student-centered learning and has a lineage that goes back to such famous names as John Dewey and Jean Piaget, and includes Carl Rogers and his approach to psychotherapy known as client-centered therapy, and Maria Montessori who established an approach to early-years education. There are two primary ideas at work here. One harks back to George Kelly, mentioned in the chapter on identity, and his personal construct theory. This approach, sometimes called "constructivist learning," acknowledges the learners' primary role in constructing meaning from experience and new information. The second idea, which seems to receive less attention, is for the teacher or coach to get out of the way and allow the learners to be reliant on their innate capacity to learn.

These two ideas are separated by a cigarette paper—but as I shall endeavour to show in the final part of this chapter, there can be a significant difference in outcome in terms of the learners developing their own authority. In the first there may well be a role for the facilitator in, say, asking questions or giving feedback. In the second there is little need for the facilitator, and if there is it lies mostly in helping the student get focused and move into flow. That is to say that in the second approach the teacher or coach has even less influence and the learner is even more self-reliant.

Awareness is Curative

Let me say more about being reliant on one's innate capacity to learn. You may recall my description earlier in the chapter on mindset and mental state, in which I describe the inner game exercise "bounce-hit". The students learned to change their grip on the racket between forehand and backhand strokes without being taught. The coach's role is solely to help the student get into a Self-Two mental state, flow. In this state people learn unconsciously because learning is hard-wired, it is innate.

Gallwey, in his book, *The Inner Game of Work,* comes up with this wonderful expression, "awareness is curative," to explain what is happening. One of his golf exercises shows what this means. The inner game coach asks the player, often a novice, to try putting—hitting a ball ten to 12 feet along the ground into the hole—and then to describe, as accurately as they can, how far the ball is from the hole. "Three feet beyond and two to the left" would be a typical response. The coach then tells the players to make no conscious adjustment but to hit a ball and again describe the result. To their surprise and delight, most people will put a ball in the hole after a few putts. Awareness, in this case awareness of the result of the action, allows the players to unconsciously adjust their technique so that the objective is met.

Changing Behaviour through Awareness

Here's another example: a number of years ago I sold a business, of which I had been the sole owner and managing director, to a mid-sized global consulting firm. The plan was that we would build up my business in their footprint. We also hired a managing director to allow me to get on with what I was then best at, namely coaching, consulting, and sales. But I really struggled. I still held a leadership role, but had no formal position from which to deliver on it—not without getting in the way of the new MD. However, I recalled Gallwey's "awareness is curative" dictum and asked myself what was the core quality of my leadership. After a little thought I came up with "inspiration". A few days later as I walked to the office, I rated my sense of inspiration. It was a four on a scale of one to ten. As I got to the main entrance of the building that housed our offices, I rated myself again at four, maybe five. The receptionist looked up and remarked that I had not been around for a while. In response I described my trip to Dubai, where we had begun some business. She thanked me and said that it was useful to know what the various businesses did and that no one really told her much.

I took a lift to the next floor, rated my sense of inspiration now at a six, and went into the office. I had almost the same conversation with the receptionist there as I had with the woman at the main entrance. There were now two ways to my desk. The one I normally took goes through a side passage, where I do not have to meet anyone, and the other goes right through the main office, where everyone sat. Without thinking I took the main office route. As I went passed a colleague's desk, she asked a question and we had a bit of a discussion. Discussion over, she thanked me, saying how useful that had been, inspirational even! And then, only then, it dawned on me: completely without trying, I had shifted my Behaviour. Awareness is curative. I use this idea to help me stay focused when working at home. I list a number of qualities that I would like to experience during the day, such as focused, joyful, or creative, and rate them at irregular intervals. Works every time.

The heart of learning is awareness. Awareness of what is. Awareness of how you desire it to be. Awareness of what is happening *en route*. Not trying, not trying to change anything, just noticing and trusting the body and mind and its capacity to learn for itself.

Learning from Experience and Intrinsic Motivation

For the moment let me state the obvious and say that both learning from within and learning from without are valid and have a place.

Teaching is important, not least because there is information that the teacher might have that the student does not. The teacher then has a choice: to let students stay with their own experiences and not interrupt the process in the hope that they will "get it" in their own time and in their own way, or to intervene and tell them.

Learning that comes from within, from experience, has a number of very significant benefits. The learners, in following their own interests and curiosity, tend to be more engaged and tend to take more responsibility for their learning and performance. It also creates a virtuous circle with intrinsic motivation. It is sourced in interest—a great start—and as the learner becomes more engaged, the enjoyment increases, feeding motivation and desire.

Daniel Pink quotes Richard Ryan, mentioned in earlier:

If there is anything (fundamental) about our nature, it's the capacity for interest. Some things facilitate it. Some things undermine it.

The learners, less reliant on the teacher or coach, begin to trust themselves more and more and thus build their autonomy and develop their own authority. Conversely, the fundamental risk in teaching, in a purely instructional sense, is that it may rob individuals of their autonomy. This can happen if the students become dependent on the teacher. And in a world in which the young are still (but only just) taught to respect their "elders and betters", this can all too easily occur. In extreme cases it can lead to kind of "learned helplessness," where students have become utterly passive and are simply waiting to be fed.

Learning, allied with deliberate practice, focused on the three other pillars—identity, mental state and mindset, and desire—is key to the flourishing of genius.

CHAPTER EIGHT

Enabling Genius in Yourself

It is my hope that in reading and reflecting on the previous chapters you will have already begun to think about how you might move forward and develop your genius. There is somewhat less science to the material in this chapter and the next; conducting the research to validate an approach to enabling genius is likely to be the next phase of the project. Nevertheless, there is nothing here that is not the subject of research or tried and tested by many hundreds of people. It is also not the intention here to write a "how to" manual, but rather to indicate some of the key areas that, in developing genius, might be addressed, developed, or learned. The first place to look in thinking about enabling is the four pillars: identifying your unique individual genius or your specific sub-genius; understanding more about your desire; and examining your mindset. But there are three other topics that require attention: getting "unstuck", or finding your autonomy; getting into flow; and what I am calling "genius thinking": making best use of your mental faculties.

Getting "Unstuck"

Mostly I meet my friend and fellow coach Peter Nolan in a pub. Such a venue seems appropriate for a conversation that might go anywhere or nowhere. Some time ago Peter told me about some work he was doing. His client was an agency that provided services to their "clients", people who were classified as "long-term unemployed." to help them back to work. On visiting one of the agency's offices, Peter noticed that the activity was centered not on the clients but on the consultants. They were active and the clients were passive. The consultants held pretty much all the power: they sat behind their desks with their cups of tea (clients don't get tea), they read in their files (clients don't get to see the files), and prescribed what should be done, right down to the smallest details. *"Remember to wear your suit." "Take the 45A bus." "Don't be late."* The clients sat meekly, nodded in apparent agreement, patronized and disempowered. At this point in the distressing tale, Peter drew a picture on a paper napkin. It was of a "stickman" clinging to the side of a cliff, terrified and utterly unable to move, fearful of even moving a finger in case it would precipitate a fall. In Peter's words: "stuck". Just like the agency's clients. Peter saw that his first task was to help these guys get unstuck. He sent an invitation to the target group of clients. At first he was told—by the consultants—that sending an invitation was not how things were done, that it would not work. Rather, you gave people the date and time and told them to be there. Peter insisted and sent out his invitation.

On the day he got a 100% turnout. He began the meeting by drawing the stickman-and-cliff picture. He saw some people nodding in recognition. Then he drew a larger-than-life angel beside the stickman. The job of the angel, Peter told them, was to rescue the poor stuck guy and put him … well, anywhere. But of course the guy would still be stuck. The clients were nodding a bit more, some laughing in embarrassed recognition. The consultants, of course, were contributing to the sticky quotient, whatever their intentions.

He gave the clients two invitations. One was to show up for the next meeting and the second was to do something, anything, differently between the two meetings as a first step in getting unstuck. At the next meeting one client told him that he always turned left when leaving his apartment, but yesterday he had turned right.

Peter's larger point is that we are all stuck, it's just that some are more obviously stuck than others. In thinking about enabling genius, an early step, if not the first, would be to get unstuck: to find your autonomy and your authority (remember the Latin root of authority means to produce, to increase, or to cause to grow). Even if this has been eroded, it is still there; all you need is 0.001% (precisely!) to get started. Once found, you inhabit it, you develop it. One way of getting unstuck is, of course, to create a pull from your desire. This will manifest differently for each of us and may take the form of a purpose, an aspiration, a dream or vision, or a goal. But it is also useful to look for "the sticky things": what keeps you stuck and immobile. What are you misconstruing that you now need to revisit, reconstrue, and then test out?

Getting into Flow

A further aspect of developing and expressing your genius is to increase your skill at getting into a flow state. Getting into flow, or Gallwey's Self Two, is not something that can be bottled and sold with a guarantee of satisfaction for every occasion. Sometimes interference emerges that is too great, like the pressure of competition or a major presentation. That said, getting into flow is a skill and, the more you practise it and the more you achieve it, the better able you will be to achieve that state in the future.

Flow also has a broader impact in enabling your genius. Irena O'Brien writes:

> *Flow, by definition, implies a growth principle. One of the conditions of flow is a balance between the demands of the task and the individual's skill level. Usually, this means that the work should be somewhat challenging. Flow is rewarding and motivates people to engage in the activity again and again and to seek increasing levels of challenge, thereby improving their skills and abilities.*

The science, and the experience of those who regularly experience flow, tells us that there are a number of things we can put in place, do, and practise that will significantly increase the likelihood of flow.

Planning and Preparation for Flow

Because the experience of flow can be so profound, many people think that getting into flow is a matter of chance—or a gift—and so don't do the work that makes it more likely. Just pitch up on the day and it will not happen. Most people I know who are expert performers plan, some with an almost obsessive zeal, for flow. Nothing is too small to be looked at and planned for—equipment (unlike the 'bad workman' pros' don't have poor tools), approach, clarity of intent and outcome, seating arrangements. In addition to the more obvious planning, they often will be mentally rehearsing a few days beforehand, visualizing specific situations or techniques, rehearsing key sentences. Irena O'Brien, in her article in the in-depth section, "The Science of Flow", refers to three "antecedents" of flow, prerequisites if you like:

1. *The goals are clear, but to be overly concerned with the goal can interfere with performance.*
2. *Feedback is immediate—knowing how well one is doing provided by the task itself or by supervisors or co-workers.*
3. *There is a balance between skill and challenge—the optimal amount of challenge is subjective, as what is challenging for one may be easy for the other.*

With these in mind, here are some of the things that are worth considering in planning for flow:
- Is the activity an expression of your unique individual genius or one of your sub-geniuses? If not, is it worth identifying the unique sub-genius for this activity? If it is, how will it impact the goals you set and your approach?
- Understand the inherent meaning in the task. What is the broader purpose in doing this?

- Identify clear performance and learning goals for the task or activity. Try to make the performance goals sufficiently challenging to engage your interest, but not so challenging or boring as to cause distraction.
- Identify your approach to the task or activity.
- Within your approach is there anything, a skill or an element of your strategy, that you need to practise deliberately to improve it?
- How are you going to rehearse?
- Finally, a key part of planning for flow is to identify any possible interferences and to find means for eliminating or reducing them.

I plan my writing activity to increase the possibility of flow—some days it happens and some it does not, but I am getting better at it. My writing genius is a "seanachi", an Irish word meaning storyteller. I try to find the story in what I want to communicate. This means identifying the basic building blocks and putting them together in a logical order so that the reader's understanding is built up, layer upon layer. It happens that I enjoy the poetry of W. B. Yeats for the rhythm in the language, so this, and a capacity to make distinctions, is what I want my seanachi to look and sound like in written words. Deliberate practice takes the form of "free writing" with a pencil on paper, writing anything that comes to mind and getting a sort of "flow of words" moving within me. To practise making distinctions I identify something, usually a concept or an idea, and ask myself repeatedly, "What is it?" and "What is it not?"

The inherent meaning in the task is most often associated with my desire to help others find their autonomy or authority and to live their lives from that source.

As I prepare for a specific writing task, I will remind myself of the elements mentioned above and then get clear about the specific intent in the piece I am to write—what I want the reader to be thinking and feeling or, perhaps, asking at the end. I will set an objective, which is usually to complete a section rather than a number of words. Then I turn off my phone and my e-mail.

Craig Walker, from the perspective of a tennis coach, one of his many roles, writes:

The champion is defined by someone who goes the extra mile, who has something that extra little bit special. They understand deeply that 100% perfection may not exist, yet they are nevertheless mindfully absorbed in a relentless quest for perfection to get as close to the 100% as is humanly possible. Equally they understand that it may not be realistic to be "in the zone" all the time, but they can certainly increase their chances of time spent in the zone by doing a number of factors:

- *They do the basics extremely well: ordinary things, consistently done, create extraordinary results.*
- *They know what they need, and have routines and teams that support and empower their performance.*
- *They are true to themselves; they are not using excess energy constantly trying to prop up their identity and be someone else.*
- *They are energy efficient; they understand that the person with the most energy wins the game.*
- *To this end they are coherent: they have a strong order of alignment in their daily living. Their clothes, their choices, and their team supports them, all fully and powerfully aligned (boat and vessel); look at the unity and power of the Djokovic camp or the Murray team.*

In my opinion, a true champion operates from a space of relaxed concentration and non-judgmental awareness. That is to say, they detach themselves from the good and the bad; rather, they are able to move beyond this into a noticing, a witnessing of their own performance. Note well that while this implies the bad shots are 'not you'—hence not to be discouraged by (it's all part of an unfolding process)—it also implies the 'good shots' are equally 'not you'. To truly get this requires great humility and poise, but I believe empowers the greatest likelihood of pure flow showing up on the court.

Following Interest

As an inner game coach, one of the techniques I might use to help someone get into flow is called "following interest". If I am with someone at the golf range, a conversation might go a bit like this:

Me   *Hit a few balls and then tell me what you notice.*
Golfer *My swing feels a bit jerky.*
Me   *Hit some more and tell what you notice this time.*
Golfer *My hips are turning.*
Me   *Hit some more and tell me what you notice.*

This sequence of questions and answers would happen three or four times and then:

Me   *You have mentioned the jerky swing, your hips turning, and some discomfort in your shoulders. Hit a few more balls and tell me which of those three things is most interesting.*
Golfer *The turning in my hips.*
Me   *Hit a few more and tell me what you notice about the turning in your hips.*
Golfer *Sometimes there's quite a lot of movement and others there's almost none.*
Me   *Ok. Tell me for each shot you take how much turning there is. Use a scale of one to five; one is almost no turning and five is a lot.*
Golfer *Two.*
Me   *Next ball.*
Golfer *Four.*

At this point the golfer is almost certainly focused and in flow or Self Two. As an inner game coach, I know that the golfer's innate capacity to learn will now kick in. My job as the coach is to get the player into flow. I do that by establishing what is being noticed, what is interesting, and then getting the player to select the thing that stands out the most. I am not directing his or her attention, but simply following where the attention is drawn. You might notice that this process as described above with the golf lesson is also the process that helps the learner access his or her innate capacity to learn. This is the process of learning through awareness, as described in the previous chapter on learning.

I think of this as a sort of continuum of attention. The first stage is "unconscious awareness": things are happening and you can be aware of them or unaware, but you are not consciously paying attention to them. As we move across the continuum, there is "noticing"; this is where you become conscious of what is in your field of attention, either as a function of choice or because the object is in itself compelling. Then there is "focused attention", where your attention is fixed on the object and there is little or no room in your attention for anything else. Sometimes this can deepen into a state of absorption—all your attention is with the object and it can feel that observer and object are one.

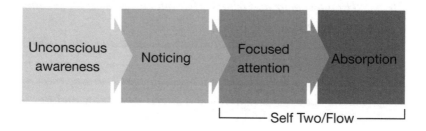

The Continuum of Attention

One way in to flow is to start to notice what's happening. This can be in almost any situation: a meeting, discussion, problem, or game. Then ask yourself what's most interesting or, sometimes an easier question to ask is, "What stands out?" and try to bring your attention to whatever that is. Then you ask yourself what is most interesting about the focus. Attention deepens; flow. In *Focus: The Hidden Driver of Excellence,* Daniel Goldman writes:

There are several doorways to flow. One may open when we tackle a task that challenges our abilities to the maximum—a 'just manageable' demand on our skills. Another entryway can come via doing what we are passionate about; motivation sometimes drives us into flow. But either way, the final, common pathway is full focus. No matter how you get there, a keen focus jump-starts flow.

As I have said, getting into flow is a skill that can be learned and developed. In his book on Psychosynthesis, *What We May Be,* Piero Ferrucci, a student of Assagioli, describes many exercises to develop your ability to focus, which is a key element, such as these:

Close your eyes and visualize the following:

A pen slowly writing your name on paper.

A single-digit number. Then substitute a two-digit one, then a three-digit one and so on until you reach the limit of the number of digits you can retain. Keep that number in front of your inner eye for two minutes.

Various-coloured shapes: a golden triangle, a violet circle, a blue five-pointed star, and so on.

And that brings me to mindfulness. I am not sure why I have such a strong objection to this word—not the practice, mind you. It sounds to me like "Buddhism lite". And anyway, I want my mind to be more empty, not full. "Full" is killing me as I try to write here in my West London office: trains, planes, fire-engine sirens, police-car sirens, construction work, and diary commitments. Rant over! Mindfulness, according to Wikipedia, *"is the intentional, accepting, and non-judgmental focus of one's attention on the emotions, thoughts and sensations occurring in the present moment, which can be trained by meditational practices that are described in detail in the Buddhist tradition."* As a mean of developing one's capacity to focus, it is excellent. There are courses everywhere, even online.

Genius Thinking

A while back, as I was thinking about this book and the possible contents, I got to thinking about the nature of intelligence and I noticed a kind of wrinkle in my thinking, something that did not stack up, a received prejudice perhaps. This was the idea that some people have intelligence, and others do not. For some reason this one did not get the scrutiny it deserved. That the few are the inheritors of intelligence is an idea that is, in large part, perpetuated by the educational system and by the unequal distribution of wealth. The ability to pay for an education or the good fortune to be selected for a great school, such as the British grammar schools of the past that then lead to "Oxbridge" or a good university, produces people that we might think of as intelligent. Again, as with so many things in this book, it's the process. The process here is the learning experiences provided by the schools and universities. I have been thinking of this as "the intelligence trick" (to borrow from the title of Baggini's book, *The Ego Trick,* mentioned earlier).

There are two parts to the trick. The first, one we have perpetrated on ourselves to our own detriment, is that we have either been tricked, or tricked ourselves, into thinking that intelligence is a given, fixed quotient—some have it and some don't. The second part is to suggest that intelligence is in some large part a trick, a technique, something that can be learned. The word intelligence itself provides a clue as to how to get started in developing intelligence: the Latin roots of the word are *inter* (between) and *legere* (to choose): to choose between. A big part of intelligence is the ability to make a distinction between one thing and another. And that is something that can be learned and practised.

The number of people I have met who think they are not intelligent is huge. In most cases it is not about some missing mental "horsepower", it is simply that they have not learned how to think. I studied architecture at Bolton Street College of Technology and an unexpected bonus was a development of my thinking ability. The process of developing a concept from a sketch to a detailed set of working drawings forced the students to resolve often-conflicting aesthetic and functional or technical problems, and the best way to do this was with a pencil and paper, drawing from different angles. In the process of doing this, one is forced into a state of absorption and focus, the surrounding world disappears, and insight comes without effort. A further aspect of thinking is that we often do not trust our thinking—we create interference. We want to know what someone else thinks, a teacher or a boss, or we simply continually second guess ourselves. I recall, many years ago, being stuck in a complex business situation without any idea about what to do and I thought, "I'll ring my father." A complete sell-out on my own capacity to think and nonsensical because my father would have had no idea what to do and was no longer alive.

Genius thinking is thinking in flow, in Self Two. Because fear and doubt are (mostly) eliminated, because there is less interference, there is greater clarity of thought. It is more intuitive and creative— when intuition or creativity is required. Genius thinking is more than cold logic, but it is that, too. It embraces and acknowledges feeling, imagination, and desire. What follows are four ideas that help induce genius thinking: the idea that thinking *unfolds;* the importance of simply *noticing;* how to *focus* your thinking and three *positions* from which to view a situation.

Thinking Unfolds

Some years back I was flying into Austin, Texas, and was looking out the window as the plane started its descent. I had been thinking about thinking and how it works, my mind slightly adrift after a long flight. I noticed the Colorado River below, taking long sweeping turns to the left and right as it made its way toward Austin and then on to the Gulf of Mexico. I was thinking, like some kind of demented engineer, about the huge waste of time and energy lost in the large meanderings of the river and that it would be far better to build a canal, straight from source to sea.

Something was knocking at the doors of my consciousness. And I kept on thinking—it dawned on me that the river was in fact following a straight line, just not one that was obvious from 30,000 feet. At ground level, if you could get far enough away to see it, you would notice that the river flowed in a pretty straight line from high to low. And you might also think that it was following the path of least resistance as it flowed around rock and higher ground rather than trying to plough straight through, almost as if the water had its own logic.

The knocking grew more persistent. What if our capacity to think had its own internal logic? What if *thinking unfolds?* Maybe we could trust our thinking, trust the process, the unfolding.

My thoughts then turned to a dear friend of mine who has struggled with depression most of her life. Every now and then she seeks help, both medical intervention and "talking therapies". With the therapy I noticed a pattern: the first two or three sessions would be productive and useful but, by the third or fourth, the value and her enthusiasm would start to diminish. I had put this down to resistance on my friend's part, unfairly. I began to see what was happening. Here's my hypothesis: in the early sessions the therapist or counsellor *had* to listen—he or she did not know the client! Value would accrue as my friend told her story, meandering as necessary, allowing her thinking to unfold. The process of thinking and talking has its own internal logic. Come the third or fourth session, the therapist would have formed an opinion, taken a position, and begun to propose a way forward, no longer listening. Let's build a canal. At which point the thinking can no longer unfold, the value of the therapy is diminished and the therapeutic relationship is undermined.

Genius requires that we trust our thinking and this means allowing it to unfold. It is by this means that we maintain the process of construing.

The Fine Art of Noticing

Noticing is the "not trying" of thinking. In the chapter on mental state and mindset, I introduced the idea of interference and stated that "trying" was a big interference. Trying in physical activities almost always induces tension and stiffness, which will lead to a performance that is inefficient, inaccurate, and inelegant. Trying to think, I discovered at school, involves frowning, pulling your eyebrows toward each other, and holding the pencil evermore tightly. Trying to write a poem seldom works. Rather you set free your imagination and let the words flow. Trying acts as a magnet for fear and doubt, and thus brings interference into the mind. Again, noticing is the "not trying" of thinking. The trouble is that, having noticed, our minds flip immediately into judgment, criticism, problem solving, or looking for an angle through which we might benefit. We don't rest with the simple act of noticing. As a consequence, we decide and act without all the information. Through resting with noticing we can inhibit the knee-jerk response, we can take the time to check out our feelings, or put ourselves in the other person's shoes. Noticing allows for greater objectivity, more distance.

Floodlight and Spotlight

There are a number of means of managing one's thinking. One is called "floodlight and spotlight". Floodlight comes first. Floodlighting sheds light on the whole territory and into every nook and cranny. It includes what one notices, what one thinks about, what one intuits, imagines, feels, and desires. Floodlight is followed by spotlight and the best question to focus the spotlight is: what stands out? Or what is most interesting? Cliff Kimber, mentioned earlier, asks this question frequently: "What do you need to think clearly about?" Spotlight. If I can find the answer, I am halfway to resolution or insight. An example of using floodlight/spotlight occurred in developing the material for this book. When faced with the problem of simplifying the material for this book, I created a mind-map on a sheet of paper that completely covered my desk and, on a Tuesday morning, I began to jot down all the things that came to mind. I then went through all my notes and then all the notes that my colleagues had created. I added all this to the mind-map. I had it in my head that I wanted, and would receive, clarity or insight by Wednesday evening. I went about various other projects, coming back occasionally to the mind-map. I started to highlight certain things and to link things together.At 5.20 on Wednesday I asked myself "from all of this what stands out?" I then saw something, a glimmer of an idea. The four pillars of genius emerged. Thinking unfolds and unfolds most elegantly in flow, when you are not trying.

Three Positions of Genius

I was introduced to this concept a long time before I conceived of the enabling genius project by a former colleague with the words: "Geniuses have been shown to have the capacity to see the world from three different perspectives—the three positions of genius." I subsequently tracked this down to some work by Judith DeLozier and John Grindler who, with Richard Bandler, were early developers of the Neurolinguistic Programming model (NLP). NLP is an approach to communication, personal development, and psychotherapy developed in the United States in the 1970s. My colleague drew a sketch of a tennis court with a small circle at one end of the court with the number "1" in it and said that position one was that of the player engaged in the game, the experience, concerned with one's own thoughts, feelings, and activities. He then drew another circle on the other end of the court with a "2" in it. He invited me to imagine that as the player, when the point was over, I could imagine looking at the situation from my opponent's point of view—I could stand in his or her shoes and imagine what he or she must be experiencing, thinking, and feeling. This is position two. From this position I might gather information about how to adjust my strategy. Finally he drew a circle with a "3" in it at the side of the court where the umpire's chair is. The umpire's chair is much taller than a normal chair, affording a good view of the whole court, the players, and the surroundings. Position three is to imagine oneself in the umpire's chair to gain an overview, to get some distance and objectivity. You might now imagine yourself in a difficult meeting such as a negotiation and being in position one, concerned about your aims and needs in the situation. You might then put yourself in the shoes of your opposite number and ask yourself: "What are their needs and aims, how are they feeling right now?" Then you might imagine yourself as a "fly on the wall" and ask yourself, "What's the dynamic here? How is the relationship between the key players?" These questions will almost certainly produce new information, allowing you to manage the meeting more effectively. This process becomes even more powerful when you combine noticing and the floodlight/spotlight technique with the three positions of genius.

As I stated at the beginning, it is not the intention to cover all, or even the larger part, of what it takes to enable genius in yourself, but rather to bring attention to some really key things: developing autonomy, getting into flow, and genius thinking. These three, combined with the pillars of genius—identity; desire; mental state and mindset—are, I believe, a firm foundation for genius.

CHAPTER NINE

Enabling Genius in Others

There are so many words that might be substituted for "enabling": coaching, counselling, teaching, facilitating, training, and many more. Each of which you could write a book about; many of those books have been written and all of these approaches are a part of enabling. But there are some ideas that are fundamental to our notion of enabling genius because of the explicit intent: to enable genius. That's clearly different from learning a new skill, say, or achieving a sales target. One fundamental is the skill of facilitating the thinking of another to raise awareness and increase understanding. Another is the ability to guide and to challenge the other's perception, and a third is the enabling relationship. These three topics are the focus on this chapter.

Facilitating Thinking to Raise Awareness and Increase Understanding

In the chapter on identity, I introduced the personal construct theory and George Kelly's use of the word "construe"—to interpret in a particular way. I have also proposed the idea that "thinking unfolds"; that there is no step-by-step process, no computer programme, that gets you to a place in your thinking predictably. Both of these processes are unique to the individual. (By the way, when I say "thinking" in the context of this book, I mean more than the purely rational. I include intuition, creativity, emotions, and even feelings in the physical sense, as all of these inform understanding and are part of the process of construing). It follows from this that the enabler's role is, in large part, to facilitate that construing, the unfolding of thinking. This facilitative approach is perhaps best known from the work of Carl Rogers, most of which was done while he was professor of psychology at the University of Chicago in the 1940s and 1950s. He started by calling his approach "non-directive", but later renamed it "person-centered". Others have called this "client-centered". While he developed his approach to be applied in psychotherapy, it has also entered into the world of education as "student-centered learning" and is seen by many as the foundation of modern-day business and executive coaching. Beyond that, increasing numbers of managers in organizations across the globe use non-directive coaching as an integral part of their management and leadership, while a major oil and gas company has transformed the safety of operations by training the safety teams in non-directive coaching techniques. Rogers himself, in his last years, used his approach to resolve political tensions in places like Belfast, Northern Ireland, and South Africa. The old authority-based, "expert"-centered approach is dying a slow and painful death (painful, that is, to the students or employees still caught up in it).

I still use the "non-directive" term because it seeks to describe the process, rather than simply act as a label. The phrase is mostly understood to mean that the therapist or coach does not direct the client or coachee; they do not instruct, tell, or advise. I think many people hold the idea in much the same way that they think of a police officer directing the traffic: telling each driver what to do. But there is a little more involved and the distinction is quite subtle. The question is what is it that is being directed—or should not be? And the answer is "attention". The fundamental idea in a non-directive approach is that where a client puts his or her attention is his or her own choice. If the therapist says, "Tell me about your current job," in that moment, if the client obliges, attention goes to where it has been directed, the current job. If, on the other hand, the therapist says something like, "Tell me what you are thinking," then the client gets to pay attention to what interests him or her and thus to allow the unfolding of their own thinking.

This should on no account be confused with the Socratic method, a questioning approach named after the Greek philosopher, Socrates, which it frequently is. In the Socratic method, there is usually a questioner who asks question that he or she already knows the answer to. In an enabling conversation, that would leave the emergent genius feeling manipulated and would undermine the relationship very quickly. In management training it is referred to as "playing Argentina". The trainer asks what is the most important produce from Argentina. The class responds with a few answers, all of which are wrong and then the trainer gives the correct answer. Power to the trainer!

Let me take a step further into the mechanics of non-directive approach. This is something that I call "following interest" and the diagram that illustrates it is called the Model T.

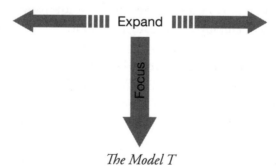

The Model T

There are two separate lines of questions that make up the T and they must follow in sequence. The purest forms are:

1. What do you notice? Or, what else do you notice?
2. What is most interesting? Or, what stands out?

In the previous chapter under "genius thinking," I wrote about "floodlight/spotlight" as a means of allowing one's thinking to unfold. The model T is another way of looking at the same thing, but is about the questions that one asks as the enabler. The enabler assists the others in bringing awareness to every nook and cranny—floodlight —and then asks what is most interesting—spotlight.

I also mentioned "following interest" in the previous chapter and used a golf lesson to illustrate the process. For convenience I represent some of that here so you can see the kinds of questions used:

Me   *Hit a few balls and then tell me what you notice.*
Golfer *My swing feels a bit jerky.*
Me   *Hit some more and tell what you notice this time.*
Golfer *My hips are turning.*
Me   *Hit some more and tell me what you notice.*

This sequence of questions and answer would happen three or four times and then:

Me   *You have mentioned the jerky swing, your hips turning, and some discomfort in your shoulders. Hit a few more balls and tell me which of those three things is most interesting.*
Golfer *The turning in my hips.*

Following interest is undoubtedly a singularly powerful way of working with others, be they employees, team members, students, clients, or emerging geniuses and there are very specific benefits that I will get to. However, a solely non-directive or person-centered approach has limitations.

Imagine the following scenario: A coaching session with a senior executive of a large, prestigious organization. The coach has diligently followed interest but the executive has not had the desired insight and the time is up, the session is coming to a close. Now the coach, in this scenario, has some experience of the executive's situation and some thoughts about how to move forward. But he is supposed to be non-directive. Does the coach call time, pack his bag and leave? I don't think so—to my way of thinking that would be unprofessional and, well, plain silly. In my 20s I had the opportunity to practise a number of times with Matt Doyle, an Irish-American tennis player ranked 65 in the ATP world rankings at his best. At that point in my life no one had told me that I was any good as a player, so when Matt said, "You should go away for six months and play tournaments. When you come back you could be top of the pile," I was completely shocked. The lack of a good mentor meant that I did not see the potential of my tennis and therefore it had not been developed (until now!). So the enabler is likely to adopt an approach that is in large part following interest, facilitating the construing, but not only that; the enabler will also help to open the eyes of the player, will challenge, point out new possibilities and shine a light on blind spots. (I have just used the word "player". I will use this word to indicate the person the enabler is working with, the emergent genius. None of the other words, such as "client", work well in this context. Coachee is a truly horrible word to get your teeth and tongue around and, worse, it carries the suffix "ee". This suggests someone who is passive and who has something done unto them (think divorcee). Player has the "er" suffix: active, the doer, and also suggests that playfulness is part of genius.)

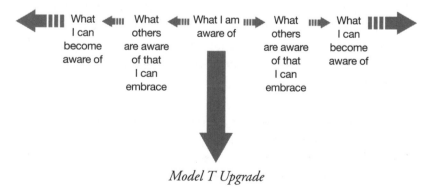

Model T Upgrade

At the center of the horizontal bar, we have what the player notices, what is in his or her attention, and this is where the enabler starts with a simple question such as, "What do you notice?" followed by "What else?" Then, further along the bar, there is what they are capable of pulling into his or her awareness, perhaps with the exercise of the imagination or with a little prompting. A question such as, "What does your intuition tell you?" or "How do you think your colleagues see this?" might be examples. Further along again, there is that which the enabler knows or has experienced that, if communicated effectively, the player can embrace. It might be more of an intervention, such as, "I am noticing a pattern, can I describe it to you?"

When all these questions have been asked, the enabler will then ask, "Of all of these, which is most interesting?" and give the choice and responsibility to the player. Ideally, I said. There will be times when what is most interesting may not be the item that will serve the player in expressing genius, so the enabler may choose to challenge that choice.

The Enabling Relationship: the Guide

Within the project team we have agreed to call the enabler the "guide". There are a number of reasons for this. The first is that it does not burden the enabler with methodologies and approaches from other disciplines that may not fit with the aim of enabling genius. It makes it clear, for instance, that the role is not solely non-directive. A guide is someone who knows the territory and, in the context of enabling genius, has trodden on much of it. This, apart from the fun, is why I have my tennis project—it doubles as a laboratory for exploring enabling genius. The guide knows the territory in the same way that really top-class golf caddies knows their home golf course. Just for the sake of clarity, caddies do a lot more than just carry the clubs. They are a source of knowledge and information, particularly about the course, distances from the call to the hole, and the appropriate club to use, among many other things. As Ted Scott, caddy to Bubba Watson, winner of the 2014 US Masters, said:

"My job is to help Bubba play his best golf."

An enabling genius guide needs to know each of the fairways, greens, and holes, things the emergent genius needs to address as he or she progresses, and a number of ways of approaching each hole. These might include coaching or counselling techniques, or exercises like guided visualization, for instance.

The "genius golf course" is different than a real golf course in that in golf the holes have to be approached in a sequence from one to 18, while the emerging genius would play the holes in the sequence that matched his or her needs, aims, and interests at the time.

Walking Before, Beside, and Behind

Reggio Emilio is an extraordinary approach to children's preschool and primary education, developed in and around the city of Reggio Emilio in Italy after the Second World War. It has subsequently been exported to many other parts of the world. The approach is very much student-centered and embraces many ideas that are congruent with enabling genius.

According to a document published by Education Scotland in 1999 it is:

A socio-constructivist model ... which states that children (and adults) co-construct their theories and knowledge through the relationships they build with other people and the surrounding environment ... it promotes the image of a child as a strong, capable protagonist in his or her own learning and, importantly, as a subject of rights.

As I understand it, a part of the way of looking at the teacher/student relationship is an inspiring notion that the teacher can adopt three different positions: to walk before the child; to walk beside the child, and to walk behind the child. To walk before the child is to lead, to guide, maybe to take the child into new areas; to walk beside the child is to engage in an activity or learning experience as a co-learner; to walk behind is to give the child the lead, to trust and let go while observing and making safe. As a way of thinking about the relationship between the enabling genius guide and the player, there is great power in this. Given that the enabler has been through the territory before and guided other players through the territory, he or she is in a position to lead—on occasions. Walking beside acknowledges that in the realm of genius we are all learners, experimenters, and scientists with a lot to learn. And in walking behind we acknowledge that with the autonomy and authority of the player, the emergent genius is paramount.

Love and Will, Again

In the previous chapter I referred to Roberto Assagioli, the founder of Psychosynthesis, and his ideas about love and will. For the sake of convenience I will present again a small part of what I wrote:

He also presented them as two opposing poles:
Will is a more 'masculine' energy and love more 'feminine'.
Will is 'head' or rational intellectual, while love is 'heart' or intuitive.
Will seeks control; love trusts and lets it happen.
Will looks for structure; love for process.

Both love and will have positive and negative aspects. Love is part of nurturing one's offspring. So is will, in providing boundaries within which the child can explore. These are clearly positive. But they also have negative aspects: an overly nurturing parent may be too protective and not allow the child to take risks or learn from the consequences of his or her actions. Similarly, an overly controlling parent, teacher, or manager may well rob the object of a child's or staff member's attention, of the opportunity to exercise their intrinsic motivation or to take responsibility. These two examples are about love and will as they show up in our relationships with others.

Love and will show up in the enabling relationship and are a key part of the dynamic. As a guide, walking before the player, my belief in his or her potential and my desire for it to be expressed may cause me to move more quickly than the player is ready for or in a direction that may not be right at the time—misplaced will. Equally my intent to "do no harm," as the Hippocratic oath has it, may result in my not challenging or giving feedback—misplaced love. In the Psychosynthesis model, as I wrote before, the intention is to find a synthesis between the two poles, to transcend and include. In the enabling genius relationship, that synthesis might be a position of some detachment, imbued with wisdom and presence.

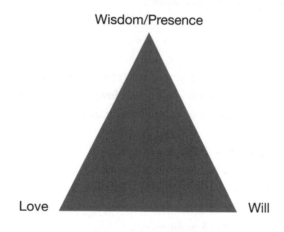

Wisdom, Love, and Will

Presence here does not mean the kind of presence that a charismatic leader might have. It is rather more quiet than that. It is about being present to what is before you, the situation, and inside you, your intentions and state of mind. Using the three positions of genius ("over here" in me; "over there" in the other; "out there" from the umpire's chair) and the floodlight/spotlight notion can help considerably here. This is now about your genius as an enabler and guide. Given the ten-year rule described in chapter two, it may take a while to become a competent guide!

The Intention of the Guide

Let's finish with the difficult bit. Why would you want to "enable" anyone? Why not stay at home, till the earth, grow vegetables, bake bread, and ferment some wine—and mind your own business. Many people coming to the enabling "game"—coaches, therapists, psychologists, and teachers, to name a few— come with the strangest mix of drives and intentions, many of which are completely unexamined and often inappropriate. The strangest of these falls into a loose category that includes the desires to heal, help, sort, save, or fix others. There is little that is more dangerous! Let me give you an example: when I was five years old my sister, Hilary, who was eight and with whom I was very close, died of leukemia. My only memory of her illness was the sense that I was not allowed into her sick room. The way I wired that one up—construed it— was that because I did not know what was happening I could not save her and as a consequence she died. And then I became an executive coach! (I was somewhat older than five when that happened.) From this you can see that my drive and intentions were primarily self-serving and therefore in danger of being in conflict with the needs of any player, particularly those with no need or desire to be saved.

Understanding one's intentions may be the hardest game in town— and the most important. Understanding is an exercise that comes in two parts. The first is to identify the often muddled, confused, and unconscious intention that it all started with and examine that for appropriateness to the situation and for congruence with one's identity. Secondly, given the probability that the initial intention is either inappropriate or incongruent, to identify the congruent and appropriate intention.

Scaling up from the critical step of identifying one's intentions— desire—in acting as a guide, the next step is to take on the whole enchilada and develop one's own unique genius as a guide.

As to why you would want to enable anyone, there is only each individual's answer. For me, enabling is something that I am moderately good at and I think of working with someone in terms of a game, a bit like a tennis match. I develop my skills, do my practice, set myself up for flow and, when the lights go green, seek to play my best game. And there is joy in that, in the performance. I would also offer this: the drive to nurture others is seated deep within our makeup as human beings. There is also a strong need, according to Maslow and Rogers, to self-actualize. Both these go hand in hand and may be reason enough, if reason is needed, to develop your enabling genius.

I am listening to T Bone Burnett as I write these last lines in my section of this book. The song is "Primitives" and the lyrics I am hearing right now are:

The frightening thing is not dying, the frightening thing is not living.

PART TWO

In-Depth and Broader Articles

It is very much the writers' intention to provide a resource, this book, from which readers can formulate their own ideas. In service of this, the purpose of the second part of this book is to provide different perspectives on some of the critical aspects of enabling genius and to bring different voices and ways of thinking to the subject. We hope this richness will provide jumping-off places for your imagination and intelligence. As I wrote in the introduction, many of the Enabling Genius team are writing in their second and even third language, and it has been a conscious decision to not over-edit the text, but to leave the character of the author, as expressed in these pages, intact.

The Relevance of Genius in the 21st Century

Richard Merrick and Andrei Mikhailenko

"The psychologist Gerd Gigerenzer has a simple heuristic.
Never ask the doctor what you should do.
Ask him what he would do if he were in your place.
You would be surprised at the difference."
Nassim Nicholas Taleb,
Antifragile: Things that Gain from Disorder

Genius is as elusive a concept as it is important.

Genius is a label that we apply; one that means different things to different people. And so we found ourselves thinking about a context for considering genius that is flexible enough to cope with most of the different meanings it may have for us.

To begin, the context itself: "the circumstances that form the setting for an event, statement, or idea, and in terms with which it can be fully understood." Perhaps one way to understand genius in context is to look at it in terms of a human timeline—when and where has it appeared, and what can we learn from that in terms of what might evoke it, what impact it has and where, and under what conditions it might appear in the future? In other words, what do the past, the present, and the future of genius tell us to make us better enablers?

The Past: What Can Be Learned from the History of Genius?

Although genius as a subject is only sporadically and often haphazardly documented, thanks to Sir Tim Berners Lee and his own particular genius it is easier than ever to bring disparate things together. To start with, we found a website dedicated to creating lists and found there a list of those people considered geniuses[1]. There are 650 of them, and fans of the site vote on them to create ranked lists. Alongside this, we pulled up a timeline of human history[2] provided by another product of the internet, Wikipedia, and overlaid the occurrence of genius to the march of human history to see what questions it might provoke.

This, of course, is hardly scientific, but with a good number of candidates on the site, it seemed like an interesting place to start. Here are some of our observations:

Genius appears to be tightly clustered.

There is an initial grouping around the time of the early Roman and Greek empires, and the foundation of some of the world's great religions. The second arises from the beginning of the Renaissance in Europe, the journeys of the great explorers, and the creation of great geographical and religious empires.

The third is centered on the industrial and agricultural revolutions in Europe, and the discovery and settling of America. There are early signs of a fourth during the first half of the 20th century, based on scientific discovery and the triggering of truly global conflict.

While, as we have said, this data is not scientific, and clearly partial (there will have been genius evident in the apparently "quiet" Middle Ages and areas of the world not discovered—but the recording of it is limited), it does provide the basis for some interesting questions:

Genius seems to be most evident at times of major, often dramatic, change. Is genius cause or effect?

Genius seems to provide propulsion for radical change. Does societal need to have a place in triggering genius?

Genius seems to happen in concentrated populations, from the dialogue of Greek Agora to the competition during the Medici period in Italy to the coffee shops of London. Does genius have a "metropolitan" factor?

Many of these areas have been considered independently, but not, to the best of my knowledge, linked together.

The Present: How Genius Can Help Us Face the Challenges of the Beginning of the 21st Century

To a large degree individuals are a product of the powerful social forces that surround them during their whole lives. First family, then school, college, employer, community, society, state—all of them carefully pass a person from one hand to another, shaping them as a useful part of their own interpretations of the "real world". Each of us can find traces of this care on our own life trajectories. It partly explains the lack of genius manifestations in our everyday lives. In most cases, we do what "has to be done," not what our genius tells us to do. What makes us do so? On the one hand, the culture of social control over individual potency, and on the other, our social consumerism, the habit to reside within a comfort zone in which we are offered ready-made roles and models of success. These two factors are so strong that they naturally intervene, even in the process of writing about genius. It is much easier to write about somebody else's genius than about one's own. In the same way, there is a temptation to explore in broad terms how relevant genius is to the challenges of the 21st century, rather than look into our own experiences at the edge of the millennium.

A decade ago, Vladimir Martynov, a modern Russian chamber and choral music composer, came up with the idea to examine major macrosocial changes in the beginning of the 21st century through the lens of personal experience. He called this process "auto-archaeology," in which all outer changes may be perceived by a person as having a certain impact on that person's "self". Then the "self" becomes an inevitable part of the change, and a story told by the person about himself or herself is at the same time a story about the macro-change in the outer world. Similar to Vladimir Martynov, we would like to explore major changes and, in particular, new challenges, which the 21st century brings to us and other people as bearers of our own inner geniuses. So what are these challenges (with which I need to balance my skills in order to remain within the "flow channel")? And how might our genius, as a way of engaging in flow, be helpful in facing these challenges?

Challenge 1: Self-responsibility

In the modern world, more independence and self-responsibility is wanted. How can we face the unknown when leaving corporate or other social "comfort zones"?

Evidence: More people are stepping off of the corporate career path. A recent study by Elance-o-Desk, an online freelance talent platform, shows that 53 million Americans are now freelancers, which is more than one-third of the American workforce. Self-employment, or freelancing, becomes a mass life model able to compete against corporate employment for large groups of the population. Moreover, there are emerging market countries, such as Vietnam, where it is estimated that 90% of the working population act as small private entrepreneurs or combine their full-time jobs with their own family-run businesses.

How Genius Can Help: Many of us dream about a future that would have us working for ourselves and doing what we really love to do. One can keep dreaming about this for years and even decades. Here one's inner genius can serve as a powerful source of energy and commitment for getting unstuck and make the decision to split with an employer. It is anxiety, fear, and other interferences that prevent us from probably the most important decisions in our lives. "Find your flow and dive into it," is what the geniuses say.

Our Personal Experiences: We both started our own first businesses at the start of the 21st century and had left corporate employment by 2008. Sometimes, when things go wrong, we find ourselves switching to the mode of regretting the corporate "paradise lost": titles, status, benefits, as well as the sense of being right in what we were doing as an organization. We belonged to a bigger whole, and the whole could not be wrong. The only problem with this idyll was that, in fact, we could not operate authentically—using our own individual genius—as a part of it. So these regrets normally fade away quickly, as soon as we recall the very atmosphere that pushed us to escape from corporations forever: standards, control, predictability, focus on stability, imposed role models, and teamwork (not bad things at all in essence!). Yes, teamwork was also there, probably because the higher in the corporate hierarchy I was, the less flow in the teamwork I could experience.

Today, at the end of our first decades of being independent entrepreneurs and coaches, we would not call it a walk on the sunny side of the street, but at the same time realize that leaving corporate careers was the only way for us to focus on what we can do best: help others make changes they aspire to. At times we find it calls on all of our different intuitions to understand what should be the next step, as there are no bosses or business consultants to tell us what to do. But, as Allen Ginsberg said once, "Follow your inner moonlight; don't hide the madness"—so we do.

Challenge 2: Unpredictability

At the beginning of the century, increasing frustration and fear were driven by the increasing complexity and uncertainty in our world. How could we cope with the unpredictable and the unknown in our lives?

Evidence: Most of the economic forecasts have proved wrong over recent years. The world experiences waves of unpredicted crises and recessions that largely influence our lives.

How Genius Can Help: As it was revealed by Nassim Nicholas Taleb, "Some things benefit from shocks; they thrive and grow when exposed to volatility, randomness, disorder, and stressors, and love adventure, risk, and uncertainty."[3] Genius is a way of engaging in antifragility (the ability to benefit from stressful factors), as strong self-identity does not change through the economic crises and other outer shocks. Since genius is all about learning (both from good and bad times), there is no negative knowledge or negative learning for a genius. Genius improves itself and gains from the unpredictable. Our inner genius is antifragile by definition.

Our Personal Experiences:

Andrei: Since the early years of this century, when together with my partners I set up Zest Leaders, a top executive talent development consultancy, we have experienced great turmoil at least twice. The latest crisis was triggered in the beginning of 2014 by the Crimea events and the Russian–Ukrainian conflict that ensued. Within just one year, as a result of the conflict, accompanied with the EU–US sanctions, the Russian economy fell into a harsh recession. Accordingly, our clients' human-relations-related budgets decreased some 50%–80%.

At the same time, our revenue increased 20% due to our "unique genius in a specific discipline" (we call it "zest"). We always introduce ourselves to our clients as partners who could help boost their ability to achieve transformative change and growth through turbulence. In the modern business world, if you cannot see evidence of turbulence, rest assured that you are in a gap between two turmoils. The gap will come to an end, but the turmoils will not (at least as the first decades of the 21st century reveal it to us).

At the organizational level, the ability to be crisis-proof will remain in high demand for a long time. Zest just got into the trend as its core competence. But do we need to cultivate resistance to the turbulently changing context as individuals? It seems that you, as a genius, can do it for you. Just let it do its job.

Richard: Like Andrei, a combination of dissatisfaction with the corporate "status quo" and a belief that there were other models of business that would offer greater satisfaction and better progress led me to form, first my own consultancy, and then together with others, GrowHouse Initiative. GrowHouse thinks of itself as an exploration consultancy. We work with people who can sense that there is a better way of working, but need to find it. We work with them, and travel with them, as they leave their comfort zones behind in pursuit of this better way of working.

It is not always easy. We often find that we need to change direction, and that the things we are looking for are not where we expected them to be. This is where a sense of genius comes in. Sensing that the path is not correct does not mean going back to a well-known path; it means trusting one's intuition to change to a different, but still untrodden, path.

We are in a time when knowledge is ubiquitous. What is known can be known to all, but what is yet to be discovered is a function of curiosity and genius.

Challenge 3: Transparency

It would not be an exaggeration to say that the previous century was the time of probably the most skilful propagandists and manipulators of public opinion of all kinds in the history of mankind. The century started with the biggest wars and ended with creating preconditions for the most scandalous, Enron-like corporate frauds. More transparency and openness is needed—and increasingly demanded nowadays to prevent new manipulations, either in politics or in business. How can we instil trust in our social life through openness?

Evidence: After a decade of shocking corporate newsmakers like Madoff Securities, Fannie Mae, or Lehman Brothers, it was found in a recent study that over half of those in Generation Z and Generation Y (the cohort of people born after 1976) state that honesty is the most important quality for being a good leader[4]. Social media is continuing to push companies to be more open and for leaders to give honest feedback and share more of their activities on a regular basis.

How Genius Can Help: Genius is based on self-awareness. Who am I, how can I make a difference, what is my intent? These are the questions being asked and re-asked many times by those engaged in unleashing their own genius. As real self-awareness is not possible without feedback from others, genius suggests a lot of sharing with others—about ourselves and our intent. The ability to be transparent is one of the key outer skills for a coach. Inner genius refines it because it finds transparency very practical. It is a practical and natural quality indeed, as is integrity (or wholeness), which saves us a lot of energy. Just imagine that each of us says what he thinks and does what he says. A utopia? Yes, but not more than genius is. The more utopias we have, the less Madoffs we get. Being honest and open for a genius-bearer is not an ethical imperative (which lies beyond the boundaries of this book), but rather one of natural qualities.

Our Personal Experiences:
Andrei: As a product of the Soviet Union and, after the breakup of the USSR, the Russian Machiavelli-style corporate culture, I still have to work on transparency of my intent to others. I wonder if others trust me, putting the "others" to the center of the question. But my genius (if I can wake it up) asks me, "Are you a trustworthy person?" (Am I transparent, reliable, and integral in what I think, say, and do?) Then the focus is shifted from "others" to my "self," and it was my genius who showed me the right direction.

Richard: The first decade of this century has taught me much. I had made a successful career through the latter decades of the 20th century by becoming expert in the business orthodoxies of the time. That ran over into the current century, but evaporated in 2008 in something similar to "a bonfire of the orthodoxies". Commitments made by a range of financial institutions proved worthless, and as a result I lost a business into which we had put much effort. I cannot blame them, or even now feel bitter (although I did at the time!). We all made choices, but the basis on which we made deals lacked transparency of intent. In hindsight, what happened was foreseeable. People and institutions made "promises" they could not keep. Genius does not do that.

Challenge 4: Transformation of Leadership
Enabling replaces leadership even in the most conservative organizations of the 21st century—banks and financial institutions. Not to mention social networks, which have no leaders by default. How shall we work with people in flow and those who are seeking it?

Evidence: The "heroic leader" era is over. Modern leaders' missions are enabling team potential through giving people more authority, implementing shared leadership, and providing resources needed for fulfilling the team's agenda, rather than giving direction and "top-down" solutions for achieving goals within the corporate vision.

Large-scale transformation of aging performance-management processes are underway. According to the Global Human Capital Trends 2015 research by Deloitte, 89% of respondents recently changed their performance management process or plan to change it within 18 months. Traditional appraisal and forced ranking do not work anymore; performance management is now a tool for greater employee engagement.

Intrapreneurship is embraced. More companies are starting to provide employees with the opportunity to develop their own initiative into a competitive product. As an example, LinkedIn has launched "[in]cubator," a program that allows any company employee with an idea to organize a team and pitch their project to executive staff once a quarter. This program is a more-evolved version of the company's "hackdays," in which employees work on various creative projects one Friday a month.

How Genius Can Help: Enabling your own genius is step one. Helping other people with their genius seems to be step two. Being a part of a "genius team" looks like step three. Do not lead, just enable —and see what happens then.

Our Personal Experiences:
Andrei: For my small business, as well as for my big family (I have five children) I still take a lot of bad leadership jobs. I used to think I needed to improve my leadership and coaching skills, until I ran across the "enabling genius" principle. Now I want to be neither a bad—nor a good—leader anymore. I focus on another thing instead: enabling genius in myself and, as a target result of it, getting the right and authority to help others with the same. I believe that this may help me make other desired changes in my life happen easier.

Richard: Much of the context of leadership was set by the business models of the 20th century. Mechanical, quasi-military command and control models dominated. As the real implications of how we work together in a highly connected economy become clear, real impact arises from working with others from a foundation of individual genius. Collaboration with others around areas of common purpose replaces yesterday's ideas of directing others to an end that was predetermined by someone else.

Examining genius' relevance to 21st-century trends is always exploring your own opportunities to unleash your genius and let others do the same for themselves. What does genius start from? Often from the ability to ask questions. Ask yourself: "What is the biggest challenge that our time brings to me? And how can my inner genius help me face it?"

The Future: What We Know about the Role of Genius Going Forward—And What We Don't Know

Genius is not always an apparent force for good. Genius seems to occur in a variety of circumstances. It does seem, though, to be a harbinger of dramatic change. So what might this ask us about the role of genius going forward?

Many would argue that the period of change we are in dwarfs anything that has gone before. The combination of the growth in human population, the impact of that on the ecosystem that is our planet, and the exponential development of technology that will, in the next 20 years, make the majority of traditional jobs obsolete, provides potent raw material for change. Whether it is for good or otherwise is a matter for an individual's mindset—of which much is written elsewhere in this book.

Perhaps the opportunity and need for 21st century genius require us to ask some powerful questions of ourselves:

When genius is a factor of "messy" human interaction, in an age when we focus on efficiency and risk aversion, how do we make space for the emergence of genius?

At a time when we educate and train people to fulfil defined jobs, how do we create the opportunity, space, and permission to pursue ideas that do not have an immediate identified return, but which may be the stuff of genius?

How do we use the capabilities of technology to increase connection? Can we use that to create the virtual spaces that mirror the informal intensity of the London coffee shops?

When it seems highly likely that traditional jobs, including the professions, are going to disappear, how do we define and promote the concept of genius as a vital component of our future wellbeing?

If we are to move from the compliance cultures of traditional organizations to the genius cultures needed for our prosperity, what will organizations of the future look like?

How do we create the "step changes" that will help us keep pace with the changes already underway?

Genius remains an elusive concept, but its power lies not in its definition, but in our awareness of its existence.

Whether it is cause or effect, random or developable, good or bad, is secondary to our need to enable it. The quality of our future demands it.

---

[1] Ranker.com – vote on the best and worst of everything.
http://www.ranker.com/list/greatest-minds-of-all-time/walter-graves

[2] Wikipedia. Timelines of world history.
https://en.wikipedia.org/wiki/Timelines_of_world_history

[3] Nassim Nicholas Taleb. *Antifragile: Things That Gain from Disorder* (New York: Random House, 2012), 3.

[4] Millennial Branding, Randstad US. *"Gen Y and Gen Z Global Workplace Expectations Study"* (September 2, 2014).
http://millennialbranding.com/2014/geny-genz-global-workplace-expectations-study/

Neuroplasticity and the Capacity for Change

Lino Pazo Pampillon and Tamara Cutrin Millan

This Is Who I Am.
"Whether You Think You Can Do It or Not, You're Right"

Imagine a child—your son, a nephew—playing tennis, winning most of his matches. Now imagine that you are the coach and have a conversation with him or his father, trying to introduce some important change to help him jump to another level, talking about his nutrition, his way of holding the racket, and hearing this answer:

"I am what I am."

Have you ever heard or said these words? "I am what I am." A short, sharp sentence, sometimes followed by "and I cannot change". Maybe this is a comforting response when we want to free ourselves from an uncomfortable discussion. On other occasions, just to indicate the limits of our age; I have already learned all I need to learn, my moment has passed, and so on and so forth. Sometimes we project our limits or expectations toward others through our prejudices, such as, "You are like that." Often we put the blame firmly at the door of our genes.

"Is It Really Genetic?"

After finishing the Human Genome Project[1] in 2003, scientists realized that we have approximately 20,500 genes, which is about the same as a mouse, and genes are only part of the story in our individual evolution. A big part is played by so-called "epigenetic" changes. Epigenetics is concerned with the chemical modifications that alter the expression of the DNA sequence; in effect, this determines how genes are expressed in response to a particular environment.

Epigenetic researchers showed that our genetics are like a piano keyboard and, depending on which key you press and how you press it, you will perform different melodies. For some this may sound like a Mozart concerto, for others like a neighbour who is still learning. Smoking, drinking alcohol, participating in sports or any other stimulus changes the expression of our genes. A ground-breaking study[2] carried out in Madrid headed by Manel Esteller (epigenetics program headmaster at The Bellvitge Biomedical Research Institute, IDIBELL) attempted to discover the differences between 40 pairs of genetically identical twins. The study concluded that differences could be traced back to the epigenetic changes forged by different lifestyles and environments.

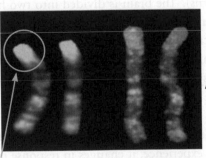

Left
Carlos & Javier
six years old

Right
Ana Maria & Clotilde
sixty six years old

Claire marks means identical genes expression,
Comparison DNA between identical Twins after years
On left six year old twins, on right 66 year old twins

He concluded: **"It has been said that DNA was the book of life, but it lacks comas, dots, etc. This is epigenetics".**

Taking this further, if it is true that we are not immutable, a slave to the DNA code that we inherited, could the same be true of our brain? Can we change it? Are you ready to be even more responsible?

The Mysterious Walnut

The human brain has always been an object of curiosity. Aristotle ventured to say its purpose was to cool the blood; Hippocrates said that its purpose was to host the mind; and Paul Broca in 1864 discovered the area in charge of language and speech. In 1890 William James spoke about plasticity to refer to the brain's modifiable Behaviour, and Ramón y Cajal developed the neuron doctrine. These were some of the pioneers who helped us better understand how this complex organ is formed, works, and how malleable and plastic it is.

Our brain begins to develop prenatally at 18 days; by 36-weeks gestation our nervous system will have developed 100 billion neurons, which continue to organize and connect throughout our lives. As adults, we have a majestic muscle, the brain, of about 1.5 Kg (the largest proportion to body weight within the animal kingdom), which consumes 20 to 25% of our total energy output (up to about 60% in newborns). The brain is divided into two hemispheres: the left, related to analytical thinking, logical and rational; and the right, more holistic, creative, and artistic. Two hemispheres integrated in one brain in which the 100 billion neurons are connected with each other through synapses. The frequency and intensity of these connections are the basis of plasticity.

"The idea of neuroplasticity is simply that the brain changes in response to our experience, it changes in response to our actions. It changes in response to our relationships. And it changes in response to specific training in which we engage. So all these kinds of activities shape the brain and we can take the advantage of neuroplasticity and actually play a more intentional role in shaping our own brains in ways that cultivate wellbeing." (R.Davidson[3])

A great example of this neuroplasticity is the story of Ramón y Cajal. A relatively low-profile student, he was able to achieve great things in his life. Speaking of these achievements he said, "If I, without the talent for science, but with perseverance and hard work, have achieved all these successes, what results could have been achieved by colleagues more talented than me?" Despite being considered devoid of genius, his perseverance, effort, and motivation helped him win the Nobel Prize in physiology and medicine in 1906 for his work that laid the foundation for modern neuroscience.

Just as epigenetics influenced by experiences impact the way our genes are expressed, so neuroscience tells us that the brain can also evolve, depending on the stimuli it receives. That means: **"We are programmed, but programmed to be unique."**

Brain Plasticity

The emergence of neuroimaging techniques have allowed us to look deep inside the brain and observe how synaptic connections build our communication networks: from fast and intuitive networks responsible for our basic reactions related to survival to slower networks devoted to our attention processes, social Behaviour as well as to our capacity to plan.

Of course these connections are easier to create when we are children, but we can create connections at any age if we learn something new. This was well demonstrated in a study at the University of Hamburg that reported increases in the hippocampus (the brain area related to learning and memory) and the nucleus accumbens (the brain area related to laughter, pleasure, and rewards) in people aged 50 to 67 after they were taught to juggle.

They were interested to see what would happen when they stopped the activity. After three months, they observed that both areas returned to their previous sizes. This has two important implications:

first, we can develop our brains through deliberate practice, but also that deliberate practice should be maintained in order to sustain the effects developed. Deliberate and sustained practice is key to creating habit.

But the brain doesn't create networks and connections just when we are learning. Sometimes it creates alternative networks and ways to survive or adapt if necessary. Ben Underwood, perhaps the most extraordinary example of echolocation ever known, whose eyes were removed at the age of two, developed the skill of orienting himself, and played basketball, rode a bicycle, and moved like any other child. He did it by developing the ability to see through echolocation. (Echolocation, as used by bats and dolphins among other animals, is the ability to locate and identify an object by emitting a sound and then picking up and processing the echo.) A big part of this ability he owed to his mother's attitude, who through stimulating his senses and a lot of determination, led Ben to better himself. Aqquaneta, his mother, was more focused on what her son could develop rather than on what he had lost. Perhaps without knowing, his mother was applying Carol Dweck's principles, explained in her book *Mindset*. This is the belief that it is indeed possible to develop our capabilities, allowing us to meet the challenges ahead.

Learning establishes new connections and the continued practice of it reinforces them and can change our brains, as was shown by Eleanor Maguire (University College of London). Eleanor demonstrated plasticity by measuring the significant increase of the hippocampus in London taxi drivers who memorized 25,000 streets over a period of two to three years. This suggests that while learning and practice itself influence the formation of synapses, it is a deliberate practice targeted to an objective that leads us to develop our brilliance.

"One of the plasticity mechanisms is the growth of new cells in the brain. When I was a graduate student I was taught that this did not occur. The brain was thought to be different from other organs in our body." R. Davidson[3]

Of course, we now know that through undertaking new activities or through deliberate practise, new cell growth occurs in the brain.

Plasticity as a Result of Attention and Emotion: If Attention Is the Door for Cognition, Emotion Is a Key to Open or Close It

Can you imagine yourself memorizing 250 orchestral works as well as the music of 100 operas? Certainly difficult if you are not interested in classical music. Toscanini (considered by many one of the best bandleaders of the 20th century) did it because of his passion for music.

It is difficult to learn something that doesn't arouse emotion. If you are not motivated—or even worse, if you feel fear—it decreases the blood flow toward the prefrontal cortex and activates the amygdale, and the capacity to pay attention is highly reduced.

Positive emotion tends to capture our attention, and blood flows in the opposite direction. We feel more connected with our skills and natural abilities. The same brain areas (thalamus, hypothalamus, septum hippocampus, amygdale, corpus callosum, and midbrain) that manage our emotional lives are also key for learning. When learning is strongly connected by emotion, learning is almost automatic, unconscious, and permanent. It is very difficult forget your first match or your first amorous liaison; perhaps you remember all the details captured by your senses (smell, touch, feelings), sure you did not need to make an effort consciously to memorize it. It just happened.

If implicit learning is automatic, cognitive learning and deliberate practice need selective and focused attention that requires more effort from our prefrontal cortex. This is not easy. A study conducted in the US found that the 47% of the time, people were not paying attention to what they were supposed to. These attention disorders, mostly caused by our modern society, hinder learning and promote the occurrence of mistakes at work, during sports, when driving and in numerous other activities.

Having a Goal Can Make the Difference

Learning something that implies positive emotions and moving to achieve our goals and objectives is important to maximize our potential. This proactive attitude activates the nucleus accumbens, rich in dopamine and essential to motivation. This positive vision determines, on a neuronal level, how long we can keep focused on an objective. We activate our ascending reticular system, and we see connections with our target everywhere. When we imagine ourselves doing or achieving something, we activate the very same brain areas as if we were doing or achieving what we had imagined.

Our skills, stimulated by implicit learning and deliberated practice and oriented to a specific goal, can transform our brain and prepare it to start a journey to maximize our inner genius.

Change to Develop your Genius

So, back to the story of that tennis player. Tony, the coach, was talking with his nine-year-old nephew, telling him that it would be better if he could change the habit of handling the racket with both hands and start to play with one. Not only that, but the hand he starts play with should not be his natural hand, his right hand, but rather his left. Tony told him that playing with his left hand would confer a significant advantage.

Imagine the player, rather than finishing the conversation with, "Ok, we will do it," instead says, "I am what I am." Perhaps without knowing this decision the coach was implementing multiple advantages[4], allowing him a more complete vision when implementing the drive, since the eye follows more widely the tennis ball. The coach stimulated his nondominant cerebral hemisphere area, increased his repertoire, and offered him a competitive advantage that only left-handers possess because information flows quicker when the predominant hemisphere is the right (controlled by the left side of the body) and those milliseconds can be invaluable when our bodies have to immediately respond to the stimuli received.

Perhaps we can imagine all these situations, but find it difficult to imagine when doing it. Tony was helping Rafa Nadal improve his brain, take advantage of neuroplasticity and neuroadaptation, and helping him become one of the best tennis players of all the time.[5]

"Not everyone is Nadal, but we all have a brain we can train." But how?

Breathe to Manage your Emotions and Increase your Attention

Our emotions are a powerful engine that can move our attention to different places—to the present moment here and now, enjoying reading this book, to our problems (a preferred place for our wandering minds), causing fear and disconnecting us from what we're doing, or trying to anticipate too much of the future and provoking anxiety. If this is the case, the amygdale, our alarm system, is activated, takes control and prepares our bodies and minds for survival reaction: fight or flight. The center of our attention is focused on the source of fear (for example, a discussion, a difficulty, or a person we dislike), even if it is caused by our thinking and there is not any risk now. Reading this book, and thinking about a problem you have, can provoke an uncomfortable reaction that captures your entire attention. If it is too significant, you can feel some effects, like increasing heart beat and blood pressure. Our bodies start to be ready as a real problem happens and this hinders prefrontal cortex functioning, responsible for planning goals and finding solutions.

Being able to manage our attention is crucial in developing our genius—distinguishing our genuine emotions and understanding the message from emotions caused by the thoughts captured by our wandering minds—can make the difference between response or reaction. The good news is that today we know how to train our attention and manage our emotions.

"If the emotion is the wind that moves the ship, emotional intelligence is the sails that guide it."

One of the more powerful techniques is mindfulness. This kind of brain exercise, based on Buddhists techniques, is proving to be highly effective both to reinforce our brain attention networks and to observe our mental life and shed some light on the deeper recesses of our minds. With a few minutes every day, we can improve our attention and tone up the vagus nerve, responsible for calmness and also for heart rate and speedy recovery after stress. This creates an optimal internal climate for attention and learning.

The Power of Meditation

It's difficult to know if Jon Kabat-Zinn, director of the stress-reduction clinic in Massachusetts, could have imagined the impact that mindfulness could have when, in 1979, he began to study mind-body interactions in relation to health. His studies are critical in understanding how meditation affects the brain, and how it processes emotions, especially under stress, as well as how it affects our health. These are the origins of mindfulness.

"Mindfulness is the consciousness which appears when deliberately paying attention, in the present moment and without judging, to how experience unfolds at any given moment." Jon Kabat-Zinn, PhD

Mindfulness consists of focusing our attention on our own breathing, posture, and includes the following specific attitudes:

Non-judgmental: Neither of our experience nor ourselves, we also learn not to judge others. When we start to truly pay attention in the present moment, we discover that we have opinions and judgments about everything and everybody.

Patience: Be open to every moment; each event has its own pace. Impatience takes us out of the present moment and distracts us from paying full attention.

Beginner's mind: Experience every moment as if it was happening for the first time; in a beginner's mind there are many possibilities, but in an experienced mind just a few.

Trust: Cultivate a deep trust in our genuine genius. It is better to try and learn from our own mistakes than to always rely on others.

Nonstriving: Too much effort causes tension; let things happen at their own course. This attitude is one of most healing, restorative, and nurturing.

Acceptance: To observe without judgment. In order to learn it is important to acknowledge one's past. Acceptance is not resignation, it is to see with clarity, helping us make better decisions.

Letting go: Do not hold on to the past, experiences or people. Learn to forgive in order to be free. Letting go is a reminder not to grasp or cling to what we want and to just let things be as they are. Letting go will save us a lot of pain and unhappiness. Letting go is the door to freedom.

Gratitude and generosity: Gratitude allows us to be aware of the wonder and abundance of the present moment and not take things for granted. Gratitude and generosity enhance our interconnectedness with one another.

Main Benefits of Meditation

The increase in the number of people practicing meditation is related to recent results from investigations and the benefits reported by people practicing it. One of the main exponents is Richard Davidson, a neuroscientist at the University of Wisconsin, Madison, who shows how we can deliberately and permanently change our brains for the better through meditation. Richard and Jon Kabat-Zinn checked the results of a group of technological company workers who were trained to meditate for eight weeks, comparing them with an untrained group. Prior to the training both groups had a greater activation of their right prefrontal areas; this area is more activated on depressed or anxious people. Once the training was over, besides feeling emotionally better, it was reported that those in the meditation group showed a larger increase in the left prefrontal area related to positive emotions.

Sara Lazar, a neuroscientist at the Massachusetts General Hospital and Harvard Medical School, is clear: "Meditation gives us the experience of serenity and concentration, which are essential for building a real self-esteem and strengthens our self-confidence."

After suffering a muscular injury in the Boston Marathon, Sara started doing yoga in order to stretch her muscles. She began to feel calmer, peaceful, and empathic, which is why she decided to change from her studies in molecular biology to an investigation about the benefits of meditation.

In her first research project, comparing long-term meditators with a control group, she detected that the meditators had a greater amount of grey matter in their insula and sensory system, the auditory and sensory cortex. As you consciously pay attention to your own breathing, sounds, and the present experience, the improvement seen in your senses is logical. She also found that participants had more grey matter in their frontal cortex, which is related to working memory and in executive decision-making. With her research she verified that, even though our cortex shrinks as we grow older and it gets harder to learn and remember, 50-year-old meditators had the same amount of grey matter as 25-year-olds.

Sara's studies showed significant changes in the brain and more thickening in four regions:

1. The posterior cingulate, which is involved in mind wandering, and self-relevance.
2. The left hippocampus, which assists in learning, cognition, memory, and emotional regulation.
3. The temporo parietal junction, or TPJ, which is associated with perspective taking, empathy, and compassion.
4. The pons, where a lot of regulatory neurotransmitters are produced.

In contrast, the amygdale, the part of the brain responsible for detecting fear and preparing for emergencies, got smaller in the group that went through the meditation program. The size of the amygdala is correlated to stress and anxiety, and a larger size is related to emotional disorders

"The exercise of mindfulness is an advance in emotional intelligence"
Daniel Goleman.

There is no doubt that new studies will be conducted and new findings will appear and some of these will modify our current view, but perhaps what won't change is what psychologists, neuroscientists, and epigeneticists are telling us today.

We are changing every day; our experiences and development depend more on our attitude than we thought. So while nature plays an important role, we are highly responsible for defining who we are and who we want to be. So the next time you answer, **"This Is who I am!"** You can add, **"Because I choose to be this way."**

Notes

[1] The **Human Genome Project (HGP)** is an international scientific research project with the goal of determining the sequence of DNA, and identifying and mapping all of the genes of the human genome. HGP remains the world's largest collaborative biological project. The project was proposed and funded by the US government; planning started in 1984, got underway in 1990, and was declared complete in 2003.

[2] Esteller's study involved more than 40 pairs of twins from three to 74 years old. The aim was to try to discover whether epigenomes were the cause of their differences. For this purpose, cells were collected and dissolved until DNA fragments were obtained. After that, those fragments were expanded until genes were detectable. www.youtube.com/watch?v=rFtvXMRNBmo

[3] *Mirabai Bush with Richard Davidson ,Daniel Goleman ,Jeremy Hunter & George Kohlrieser ,Working with Mindfulness, Research and Practise of Mindful Techniques in Organizations, MORE THAN SOUND Kohlrieser.*

[4] According to eye and body side dominant, athletes can be crossed, where the dominant eye is on a different side of the body than the dominant foot or arm. Athletes can be also homogeneous, where the dominant eye and foot or arm is on the same side. Concerning the brain, the optimal for a tennis player is being crossed, since when implementing the drive, the shot vision is more complete since the eye follows more widely the tennis ball.

[5] Coba Rosa "Rafa Nadal, la excelencia de la plasticidad cerebral" –"Rafa Nadal ,the excellence on brain plasticity" , Perarnau Magazine 20 , October 2013 http://www.martiperarnau.com/saluddeportiva/rafa-nadal-la-excelencia-de-la-plasticidad-cerebral/

The Science of Flow

Irena O'Brien

Is flow central to the idea of delivering peak performance and enabling your genius?

Mihaly Csikszentmihalyi is a pioneer in our understanding of peak performance, creativity, and human fulfilment. He has encompassed these within the notion of something he termed "flow"—a joyous state of heightened focus and total immersion in activities such as art, sport, science, or work. This article summarizes a range of scientific studies into flow. It demonstrates that being able to create a state of flow is critical to peak performance and enabling our own individual genius.

Csikszentmihalyi studied flow in a broad variety of occupations, from artists and chess players to business leaders, and from ordinary people to the elite. His research and that of many others found that flow is a rewarding experience; it provides the means for people to live up to their potential and is a predictor of higher performance —or "being in the zone"—in a wide variety of domains, from work to leisure to creative pursuits. Flow drives individuals to creativity and outstanding achievement and is the key to living a meaningful life (Csikszentmihalyi, 1990).

While flow is not rigidly defined—in fact Csikszentmihalyi warned against this—it does nevertheless have a number of distinct elements, all of which are open to measurement (see the section, "Antecedents and components of flow," below) and therefore scientific study. In reviewing the literature, I have, therefore, cast a wide net and included research that is correlated with flow but which the researchers call by a variety of names: inner work life, employee attitudes and engagement, intrinsic motivation, work enjoyment, and task absorption. Bakker (2008), for example, showed that intrinsic motivation, work enjoyment, and task absorption are all highly correlated with an independent measure of flow.

The remainder of this article covers the following:

- How flow appears in our lives and how it benefits us all.
- The key elements of flow, in more detail, and the conditions for its creation.
- What recent neuroscience has discovered about what is happening in our brains during flow experiences.
- Finally, what can happen if we take flow too far.

Flow at Work
Flow is more often experienced during work than in leisure activities (Csikszentmihalyi and LeFevre, 1989). At work, it enhances people's creativity and productivity, corporate performance, and even shareholder value.

One of the most comprehensive and detailed studies of how flow in the workplace contributes to optimal performance is that of Teresa Amabile and Steven Kramer (2011). They wanted to know what happened to people's thoughts, feelings, and motivations as they worked on solving complex problems. They recruited 238 knowledge workers in 26 project teams in seven companies in three industries, from small start-ups to well-established companies. Every workday for about four months, the workers answered questions about their inner work lives (i.e., perceptions, emotions, and motivations) during the day and described an event that particularly stood out during the day. There was a 75% response rate, resulting in 12,000 individual diary reports.

After examining all of the diary reports, they found that when people had a positive inner work life, they were more creative, more productive, and more committed to their work. They also found that progress in meaningful work, no matter how small, significantly influenced the participants' inner work lives, leading to an upward spiral that they called the progress loop. This is important to companies because their bottom line depends on the performance of their people.

Flow also has a positive impact on corporate financial performance and corporate value (i.e., future stock returns: Edmans, 2012). Harter, Schmidt, Asplund, Killham, and Agrawal (2010) examined longitudinal data collected by Gallup, Inc., a global research and consulting organization. The data they examined comprised 2,178 business units with 141,900 employees in ten organizations, ranging from retail stores and manufacturing plants to hospitals and sales offices. They found that employee attitudes and engagement had a causal impact on customer loyalty, employee retention, sales, and profit. In addition, of the 12 questions on their employee attitude and engagement questionnaire, question #3: "At work, I have the opportunity to do what I do best every day," a clear indicator of flow, had the strongest causal impact on financial performance.

Flow and Learning

Flow, by definition, implies a growth principle. One of the conditions of flow is a balance between the demands of the task and the individual's skill level. Usually, this means that the work should be somewhat challenging. Flow is rewarding and motivates people to engage in the activity again and again and to seek increasing levels of challenge, thereby improving their skills and abilities.

The contribution of flow to learning has been well studied in sports and education. Two of the classic studies on flow and learning are those of Schüler and Brunner (2009) and Engeser and Rheinberg (2008). Schüler and Brunner assessed flow during training for a marathon race and found that runners in flow trained harder than those who were not in flow, and had faster race times. In an educational environment, flow predicted better exam performance both in a required statistics course and in a foreign language course taken voluntarily (Engeser and Rheinberg).

Flow of Innovation and Creativity

Csikszentmihalyi (1990) originally set out to study how people felt when they most enjoyed themselves and why. One of the first groups of people he studied were creative experts—artists and musicians—and found that creative behaviour is often characterized by the flow state. So creativity and flow are intimately related.

In the workplace, flow has been found to enhance creativity. Amabile and Kramer (2011) in their large-scale study, found that intrinsic motivation, or deep engagement in the work, led to work that was more creative than work that was extrinsically motivated. And workers continued to be more creative for several days later. Flow also leads to employees taking on extra roles, such as making constructive suggestions and looking for new ways to improve efficiency (Eisenberger, Jones, Stinglhamber, Shanock, and Randall, 2005).

There is a close relationship between flow and positive mood and emotions. In fact, Csikszentmihalyi defined the characteristics of flow by asking subjects to describe enjoyable activities or experiences. Amabile and Kramer (2011) found that on the days that employees experienced a positive mood, they were 50% more likely to have a creative idea. They also found the reverse effect; that creativity leads to joy. In their report, they state that this relationship applies to all dimensions of performance.

Flow in Teams

Recent research shows that flow impacts the performance of teams. Two recent studies (Aubé, Brunelle, and Rousseau, 2013; Heyne, Pavlas, and Salas, 2011) have used business simulation games to investigate if flow impacts team performance. They have found that the combined flow experience of team members predicted team performance such that when flow was higher, team success was higher. They also found that flow was related to the team's goal commitment, the extent to which members shared information, team cohesiveness, and team knowledge building.

Conditions of Flow

From his years of research, Csikszentmihalyi identified nine components of flow that apply regardless of the activity, be it creative, leisure, or work. He stressed, and research confirms, that flow should not be rigidly defined—not all of the components inevitably accompany flow, and their relative importance may vary depending on the task (Csikszentmihalyi, 2003). During flow, people feel a deep sense of enjoyment (Csikszentmihalyi, 1997) and that may be a key indicator that the person is in flow.

Antecedents and Components of Flow

1. The goals are clear, but to be overly concerned with the goals can interfere with performance.
2. Feedback is immediate—knowing how well one is doing is provided by the task itself or by supervisors or co-workers.
3. There is a balance between skill and challenge. The optimal amount of challenge is subjective; what is challenging for one may be easy for another.
4. Concentration deepens and distractions are excluded from consciousness.
5. The present is what matters; when deeply engaged in a task, the worries and problems of everyday life fall away.

6. We feel in control of the situation; we know what to do and there's no worry of failure.
7. Sense of time is altered. When deeply engaged in a task, we lose our sense of time; it seems to fly by or slow down.
8. Self-consciousness disappears. When immersed in an activity, anything not directly related to the task at hand, including the self, is pushed out of consciousness.
9. The activity becomes autotelic: the joy of working is more important than extrinsic rewards.

The first three components—clear goals, immediate feedback, and balance between challenge and skill—are considered to be antecedents or prerequisites of flow. They must be present for flow to occur. The last six components are considered to be expressions of flow. They may or may not occur and they are what bring enjoyment to the task (Moneta, 2012).

Optimal Challenge-Skill Balance

Probably the most researched component of flow is challenge-skill balance. Flow occurs in the space between anxiety and boredom: if the task is too challenging, the person will experience anxiety; if the task is too easy, the person will experience boredom. Flow is not possible when we are anxious or bored.

The level of challenge is subjective: what one person may experience as just the right amount of challenge, another may experience as too much or too little. But Csikszentmihalyi (2003) writes that ". . . any activity can produce flow, because hidden in even the most seemingly mundane tasks—working on the assembly line, talking to one's child, or washing dishes—are opportunities for using one's skills".

Csikszentmihalyi (2003) describes a worker in flow slicing salmon day after day, a seemingly mundane job. "He described how every fish he picked up was different from its predecessor. He would hold the fish by its tail and slap it against the marble counter, looking at it and feeling it ripple until he developed a three-dimensional mental x-ray of its anatomy. Then he would pick up one of his five knives—which he sharpened to perfection several times a day—and go about the business of slicing the fish as finely as possible with the fewest moves, discarding the least amount of good meat." This is an example of how even the simplest task can be transformed into a complex, satisfying activity by giving it a high subjective value.

Other Factors that Influence Flow

The experience of flow is not the same for everyone. In fact, people vary in their ability to experience flow. Levels of anxiety prior to the occupation, the degree of challenge an occupation presents, thought or the absence of thought during the flow experience, and the meaning of the occupation all affect the experience of flow (Wright et al., 2007).

The ability to experience flow is also governed by our motives. Our basic motives are achievement, power, and feeling that we belong, which may be implicit or explicit. Implicit motives are unconscious motives that determine our focus and Behaviour. Explicit motives are those we are consciously aware of. Both coexist in an individual and are generally widely independent of each other (most research show zero correlation between the two). To experience flow, implicit and explicit motives must be in agreement with each other. The optimal challenge-skill balance, for example, would speak to those with an implicit achievement motive, but not to those with an implicit power motive or needing to belong because they're not motivated by pure achievement. That does not mean, however, that they won't achieve, but rather that their motivations for achieving would be for reasons of feeling powerful or feelings of belonging.

Whether the individual is action-oriented or state-oriented will affect the ability to experience flow. State-oriented individuals quickly get

tired or bored with an activity and have difficulty maintaining concentration. Action-oriented individuals can become deeply engaged
in a task and will persist with complete absorption (Baumann, 2012).

Other Conditions and Requirements
Intrinsic Motivation

Engaging in a task out of interest or enjoyment for its own sake,
or without any external incentive or reward, is highly related to
flow (Csikszentmihalyi and LeFevre, 1989). By definition, flow
is understood as an intrinsically motivating state; in fact, some
researchers have conceived flow to be a model of intrinsic motivation (Landhäußer and Keller, 2012). Moreover, individuals who
experience a challenge–skill balance in a task are more likely to freely
choose to reengage in that task, a behavioural indicator of intrinsic
motivation (Fong, Zaleski, and Leach, 2014). And extrinsic rewards
can even reduce creativity in certain circumstances (Baer, Oldham,
and Cummings, 2003).

High intrinsic motivation tends to lead to higher levels of creativity
because such individuals tend to be excited and enthusiastic (Amabile and Kramer, 2011). But work-related activities are generally
extrinsically motivated and if employees do not perceive their own
competence, autonomy, and performance in a positive manner, it's
more difficult to experience flow. Under cognitive evaluation theory
(Deci and Ryan, 1985), intrinsic motivation comes from feelings
of competence and autonomy. Extrinsically motivated activities can
eventually become intrinsically motivated by helping employees feel
competent. Inherent in every task is feedback, and just the right
amount of challenge can generate feelings of competence.

Work Environment and Design

Certain work environments contribute to the likelihood of flow. The
research identifies supportive team leaders, work that is challenging

and allows for autonomy (decision latitude), the ability to use creativity and a variety of skills, and the opportunity to learn new skills as important for experiencing flow. "Good managers realize that one of their main tasks ... [is] ... to provide increasing variety and challenge to their workers, so as to prevent their stagnation." (Csikszentmihalyi, 2003, p. 65).

Fagerlind, Gustavsson, Johansson, and Ekberg (2013) surveyed 3,667 individuals in a wide variety of occupations (i.e., nurses, engineers, eldercare workers, social workers, teachers, cleaners, and administrative staff) from nine organizations, both public and private. They found that individuals with a greater amount of autonomy (the opportunity to influence work activities, use creativity and skills, and learn new skills) had more flow experiences (see also Fullagar and Kelloway, 2009).

In a 2013 McKinsey report, the business leaders surveyed voiced that the largest impediment to peak performance of employees was lack of meaning. Amabile and Kramer (2011, p. 74) found that "... making progress in meaningful work is the most powerful stimulant to a great inner work life." Csikszentmihalyi (1990; 2003) has written extensively about the importance of meaning. He writes about meaning in the sense of "turning all life into a unified flow experience ... so that one can approach optimal experience as closely as humanly possible" (1990, p. 214). And "... to inspire workers to give their best to their work ... an overarching goal that gives meaning to the job [is needed], so that an individual can forget himself in the task and experience flow without doubts or regrets" (2003, p. 143). He identifies two kinds of meaning: the meaning that governs one's life, and the meaning attached to one's work. In order for workers to give their best, these two meanings need to be in agreement with each other.

Work stressors can either spur employees to give a better performance or hinder it. Challenge stressors are those stressful demands viewed as obstacles to be overcome in order to achieve goals. Hindrance stressors are stressful demands viewed as arbitrary and stand in the way of performance. In a meta-analysis of studies on work stress and performance, LePine, Podsakoff, and LePine (2005) found that challenge stressors predicted motivation and performance, whereas hindrance stressors negatively impacted performance and motivation. This is further supported by Amabile and Kramer (2011), who found that low to moderate time pressure—challenge stressor—was a good thing for creativity. And sometimes meeting a deadline for an important project also spurred creativity. This was different from a constant time pressure—hindrance stressor—which had a negative effect on creativity.

Organizational and Leadership Characteristics

Csikszentmihalyi (2003) writes that creating an organization that fosters flow requires a commitment from top management. We've already seen how flow is good for companies. There are many leadership styles and the question is which leadership style encourages workers to experience flow. The research shows, overwhelmingly, that transformational leadership has a positive influence on work-related flow. Transformational leaders, through their vision, generate enthusiasm, energy, and commitment in their workers and inspire them to perform beyond their expectations (Schiepe-Tiska and Engeser, 2012). Transformational leadership not only contributes to intrinsic motivation, flow experiences, work satisfaction, and corporate loyalty, but also to the organization's financial performance.

Barrick, Thurgood, Smith, and Courtright (2014) found that CEO transformational leadership fosters the perception that every worker is an important part of the organization and emotionally invested at work, which they called "collective organizational engagement". They surveyed 900 workers at all levels of the organization, including top-level management, from 83 small- to medium-sized credit unions in the US and found that collective organizational engagement was positively related to firm performance, measured as ROA (return on assets).

One of the business leaders that Csikszentmihalyi (2003) interviewed for his book, *Good Business: Leadership, Flow, and the Making of Meaning,* was J. Irwin Miller, then chairman and CEO of Cummins Engines. During his tenure, Miller had taken the company from a local operation to a Fortune 500 company with operations around the world and had this to say about the role of a leader: ". . . the head of a business is an enabler rather than a doer" (p. 107).

One of the things that a leader can enable is flow. It's well known that emotions can cross over from one person to another. This is called emotional contagion and the question was whether flow could also be contagious. In a study of 178 music teachers and 605 music students from 16 different schools, Bakker (2005) found that flow crossed over from the teachers to the students. That is, students "caught" the flow experience from their teachers. This study shows that leaders in flow, in addition to setting an example of flow, can "infect" their workers to have more flow experiences.

Lastly, Teresa Amabile's research (Soriano de Alencar, 2012) found that the following characteristics of organizations promote creativity:

1. Freedom regarding the means available to reach the goal;
2. Sufficient resources: facilities and information, and time to explore, mature, and develop ideas;
3. Balance between challenge and skill;
4. Encouragement and recognition by supervisors;
5. Recognition and support by top leaders of the organization.

Neurophysiology of flow

One of the effects of flow is a feeling of effortlessness. An important question is whether the feeling of effortlessness is a subjective feeling or whether it can be seen objectively.

Neurophysiology of Flow at Work

One way to measure cognitive effort is by looking at brain activations and deactivations while participants are in flow. But, because it happens suddenly, flow is difficult, if not impossible, to catch in work environments (Ceja and Navarro, 2012). Consequently, neurophysiological research has often used video games and exercise to investigate flow, because they reliably lead to flow and can then be investigated in real time.

A common misconception is that the prefrontal cortex, located behind the forehead and responsible for planning and decision-making, is suppressed during flow (Dietrich, 2004). This suppression of the prefrontal cortex is called transient hypofrontality—hypo (meaning slow) is the opposite of hyper (meaning fast). But the transient hypofrontality hypothesis was proposed for highly practiced tasks, such as video gaming and athletic performance. Video games, for example, are hardly reflective of the real world and can often be played mindlessly; Shulman, Fiez, Corbetta, and Buckner (1997) found that transient hypofrontality is commonly seen in studies using video games.

But one can experience flow even during tasks that are not highly practiced. More recent research has found that the prefrontal cortex continues to be involved during flow while performing more complex tasks. Ulrich, Keller, Hoenig, Waller, and Grön (2014) looked at the brain activations of participants while they were performing mental arithmetic in flow. They found that, rather than an overall transient hypofrontality, brain resources were reallocated from certain frontal structures to other frontal structures. The medial prefrontal cortex, implicated in thoughts about the self, showed decreased activation and the left ventro-lateral prefrontal cortex showed increased activation, which reflected a deeper sense of cognitive control.

Another way of measuring cognitive effort is by looking at brain waves when participants are in flow. Beta waves (13–30 Hz) are associated with higher vigilance in a task whereas alpha waves (8–12 Hz) are slower waves associated with a calm, alert state of mind, and also with increased attention and cognitive control.

Given the difficulty in catching flow at work, there are few studies that use real-world tasks. The study by Léger, Davis, Cronan, and Perret (2014) used a good example of a real-world type task. They asked participants to play a computerized business-simulation game using enterprise resource planning (ERP) software. In this game, the participants make critical business decisions and proactively manage day-to-day operations of their company while competing against other companies in the same market. They found that frontal brain waves changed as the task progressed: beta waves were observed early in the game and decreased with increased levels of flow. As the participants progressed in the task and experienced more flow, they became more comfortable and confident in the task and the participants' brain waves shifted from beta to the slower alpha waves. Study participants who reported higher levels of flow showed high alpha and low beta during flow. This study indicates that brain activations change as a task progresses and that cognitive effort decreases as participants experience more flow.

So, rather than an overall hypofrontality, or suppression of the prefrontal cortex, during flow, the prefrontal activations change as a task progresses. The early stages of flow are characterized by more self-reflective thinking and higher vigilance, hence more cognitive effort. When more deeply in flow, the brain shifts to a calmer and more alert state of mind, together with a deeper level of cognitive control.

Stress can also be used to measure whether the feeling of effortlessness during flow is subjective. Both heart rate (HR) and heart rate variability (HRV) are measures of cognitive effort. HRV is a measure of the beat-to-beat changes in heart rate. Even though we measure HR as beats per minute, heart rate is not regular, but changes from beat to beat. The inhalation activates the sympathetic nervous system, responsible for the activation or acceleration response during stressful situations. The exhalation activates the parasympathetic nervous system, responsible for the deactivation or deceleration response during a resting state. The higher the HRV, the greater the state of relaxation and the lower the HR. If flow is accompanied by a feeling of effortlessness, HR should decrease and HRV should increase. That is exactly what Léger et. al. (2014), described above, found.

Peifer and colleagues (2014) suspected that the relationship between HRV and flow was not linear. They used the computer program Cabin Air Management System (CAMS), which required participants to manage the complex environment of a simulated spacecraft's life-support system. In order to test the limits of HRV during flow, they recreated real-life working conditions by inducing a moderately stressful environment using a simulated job interview, characterized by asking unpleasant questions and refusing to give answers to interviewees' questions. To keep stress levels high, participants were also told that the CAMS would predict future job success.

They found an inverted U-shaped function between the sympathetic, or stress response, portion of HRV and flow. Lower and higher levels of the sympathetic portion of HRV were related to lower flow, but moderate levels of the sympathetic portion of HRV were related to higher levels of flow. Cortisol, a hormone released during stressful situations, also showed an inverted U-shaped function, but only for the first half of the task, where moderate levels of cortisol predicted higher levels of flow. There was no relationship between cortisol levels and flow during the second half of the task. These results show that there is a moderate level of arousal during flow; therefore we can say that flow is not entirely effortless.

Dopamine, a neurotransmitter released during rewarding activities, is involved in learning, reinforcement of behaviour, attention, and motivation. Flow is an enjoyable experience and should be accompanied by the release of dopamine, but the research is scant. Koepp, Gunn, Lawrence, and Cunningham (1998) found that the release of dopamine increased when participants were playing a rewarding video game, and this release was related to their performance in the game. de Manzano, Cervenka, Jucaite, Hellenäs, Farde, and Ullén (2013) found that individuals more predisposed to flow experiences have more dopamine D2 receptors than individuals who are less predisposed to flow, suggesting that flow proneness may be partly biological.

Neurophysiology of Creativity

The hallmark of creativity seems to be high alpha levels, or a relaxed, alert state of mind, together with activation of the default mode network (when focusing inward).

The default mode network (DMN) is a set of brain structures, including medial frontal structures, that are deactivated when performing a task. The cognitive control network (CCN) is a different set of brain structures, including lateral prefrontal areas, that is active while performing a task. During the process of creativity, the DMN and CCN create a cycle that reflects the cognitive process involved. In essence, during creation our focus is inward (DMN) and during testing our focus is outward (CCN) (Jung, Mead, Carrasco, and Flores, 2013). This is additional evidence that, rather than an overall transient hypofrontality, brain resources are reallocated during flow.

In a review of studies on creativity, Fink and Benedek (2012) consistently found that creativity is accompanied by an increase in alpha levels in frontal areas. As we saw above, alpha waves reflect a calm, alert state of mind. The alpha power was related to the creativity level of individuals (the more creative individuals had higher alpha power) and the requirements of the task. Interestingly, they found that creativity and frontal alpha could be trained by exposing people to other people's creativity or positive emotions and by verbal creativity training using computerized creativity problems such as inventing names, finding slogans, or finding nicknames.

Alpha waves are also associated with insight. Insight is different from creativity in that it is the sudden knowing, an "Aha!" moment. Kouinos and Beeman (2009) investigated the neurophysiology using complex word-association problems. In the two-second period while participants waited for the problem to be presented, the participants who used insight to solve the word-association problem displayed more alpha activity over occipital regions than participants who used analytical reasoning to solve the problems. Indeed, this pattern is so robust that the authors can predict who will solve the problem using insight by looking at the participants' brain waves in real time. This suggests that, to encourage insight, we need a calm, alert state of mind.

Downsides of Flow

"Flow experience, like everything else, is not good in an absolute sense" (Csikszentmihalyi, 1990, p. 70). Because flow is so intrinsically rewarding, it can create the motivation to seek out more flow experiences, purely for the rewarding feelings associated with flow, potentially leading to addiction and risky behaviours.

How flow can lead to addiction and risky behaviour is through operant conditioning, a well-studied and powerful learning mechanism in psychology. Operant conditioning is a learning process that uses reinforcement to change behaviour. Flow is a rewarding experience and, according to the rules of operant conditioning, rewarding a Behaviour increases the likelihood of repeating that behaviour. In one study, Olds and Milner (1954) implanted electrodes in the brains of rats. To stimulate the release of dopamine, a neurotransmitter that is released during rewarding experiences, the rats pressed a button. They found that the rats would continually press the button to stimulate themselves, to the point of ignoring hunger and thirst.

Extreme sports and internet use are activities that can easily evolve into addiction or dependence. In extreme sports, participants report a state of euphoria when engaging in the sport. In at least one study (Partington, Partington, and Olivier, 2009), big-wave surfers have even used the term "addiction" to describe their peak experiences. In addition, they often exhibit tolerance (the need to continually increase speed and levels of risk to experience flow), and withdrawal (depression when not able to engage in the sport). Thatcher, Wretschko, and Fridjhon (2008) also report similar evidence of tolerance and withdrawal in problematic internet use. They found that the stronger the participants' flow experience, the more problematic their internet use.

Risky behaviour is not limited to extreme sports, but can be found in many other occupations. Successful trading on the stock market, for example, is rule-based. No matter which rule traders follow, the most important rules spell out when to get out of a trade. But, "[t]raders who have just made some successful trades are more likely to take subsequent risky trades" (Steenbarger, 2003, p. 50).

It is worth giving a word of caution to highlight that some advocates of flow promote extreme versions of achieving it. They often come from a high-adrenalin, extreme sports background and use a high-adrenalin sports model of flow. They advocate a form of flow that can easily lead to addiction and use terms such as "flow hacking" (which refers to a shortcut into flow) to describe this. They spread information that's just plain wrong and may even be harmful: they use terms such as "addictive"; that after a lot of flow one can get deeply depressed (as we have seen above, this is a symptom of addiction); and that training in flow on the ski slope will lead to work flow (for most of us, flow is a state, therefore context-dependent). The old adage is true: if it's too good to be true, it usually is.

Csikszentmihalyi (1990) was well aware that flow is not always positive. He warned us to ". . . learn[ing] to distinguish the useful and harmful forms of flow, and then make[ing] the most of the former while placing limits on the latter" (p.70).

Conclusion

We've seen how flow enhances employee productivity and creativity and impacts corporate performance. An example of how flow can significantly affect results is my client, Rob. Before participating in flow training, Rob was good at prospecting but poor at closing sales. The one thing that he needed to do to be able to close sales was to lose his self-consciousness when asking for the sale. During flow training, Rob learned how to place himself into a confident, sales-closing state. His sales not only tripled in the six months following the training, but he met his projection for the entire year during that six-month period.

Models of Flow

Caroline Cryer

What Is It?

Flow is often conceived of as having some common traits, perhaps with a personal application. The proposition here is it is a state—a way of feeling and being for a period of time. The literature and research on the subject generally indicates we are at our best, do our best, and deliver the best results when we're in this "flow" state. Most scientific breakthroughs, progress in the arts, and innovative breakthroughs emerge from flow states.

However, getting into it is tricky and getting out of it is really rather easy. I like to think of it a bit like going for a run. We find distractions, are seduced by alternative options, and struggle right up to the moment we're putting our trainers on. And then once we're outside, the fresh air starts pumping in to our lungs, we feel amazing (usually!) and wonder why we don't do it more often!

In flow, we are so immersed in the moment, nothing else really features. Action and awareness merge. Time flies. Performance improves. Awareness of what you're actually doing seems to evaporate. In flow, every action, each decision, leads effortlessly, fluidly, seamlessly to the next.

Harvard Medical School psychiatrist Ned Hallowell explains it: "Flow naturally transforms a weakling into a muscleman, a sketcher into an artist, a dancer into a ballerina, a plodder into a sprinter, an ordinary person into someone extraordinary. Everything you do, you do better in flow. From baking a chocolate cake to planning a vacation to solving a differential equation to writing a business plan to playing tennis to making love. Flow is the doorway to the 'more' most of us seek. Rather than telling ourselves to get used to it, that's all there is, instead learn how to enter into flow. There you will find, in manageable doses, all the 'more' you need."

How Do You Get It?

So flow is something we can stumble across, but with its resultant increase in performance, it stands to reason we would want to access it more often and more easily. The good news is, research suggests there are ways you can practise getting in to flow quicker. Without practice and focus, it is hard to turn it on at the click of a finger. And, as we've been told since we were children, practise makes perfect! The incentive being, the research indicates significant improvements in productivity. In Steven Kotler's *Forbes* article, "Tips for Finding Flow: a High Performance Users Guide for the New Year," The suggestion is for senior executives this could be a five-fold increase. Kotler from the Flow Genome Project suggests there are five things we can practise to achieve flow more regularly:

(ref http://www.forbes.com/sites/stevenkotler/2015/01/01/5-tips-for-finding-flow-a-high-performance-users-guide-for-the-new-year/#2715e4857a0b3dc5d6c44992)

1. Take a risk; being able to suppress the fight-or-flight response can drive you into flow because the dopamine produced drives focus.
2. Actively recover: at least once a week ensure you get eight hours of sleep as well as adding two 30–60 minute active recovery sessions. Kotler suggests sauna, massage, or just a couple of naps.
3. Focus: lock your focus on the present moment. Using some of the now readily available mindfulness and breathing techniques can help.

4. Prioritize passion: passion drives focus because, simply put, we pay more attention to what we care about, which in turn creates flow. By dedicating time to the things you love to do and blocking out distractions, the passion for the activity feeds the flow.

5. Read: Kotler advises we do this four times a week because dopamine (the flow-inducing brain chemical) is released during pattern recognition and we need new information (gained from reading) to find the patterns.

Mindfulness meditation evangelists would probably agree a regular meditation practice also enables a faster route into flow. An increased appreciation for shutting out distractions, emptying your mind of the constant chatter and interrupting thoughts, and remaining present and in the moment probably all contribute to accessing a flow-state.

Despite all this, flow can still be elusive. You viscerally know when you're in it, but not necessarily how you got there, nor perhaps how you lost it. Reliably reproducing the state on demand seems to be the magic bullet we're searching for.

It's easy to look to the world of sports to observe how flow impacts genius. Athletes appear to be able to access it more often and more easily—why is that?

I have recently taken up learning a new sport. Coming from a triathlon background, and focusing more recently on cycling, I started to pay attention to the fact great triathletes/cyclists in my local club tended to come from rowing. What is it about rowing that nurtures great future cyclists? Is it the muscles, the endurance, the ability to take a visit to the "pain cave" and stay there?

So in a bid to improve my cycling, I've taken up rowing. Everything about learning a new skill as an adult has been brought under the microscope. The frustration of watching others doing it well and not being able to translate that into individual performance has been a key lesson. As has paying attention to how I learn best and how to harness when I'm getting it right in order to recreate it. Our coach has a wonderfully kinaesthetic style to his explanations, connecting us to the visceral feeling of sending the boat through the water. This got me thinking about flow; how I access it and how I lose it.

Flow in rowing is as descriptive as it is instinctive. The boat flows through the water, but only when rowed well. Water is passive; it will flow where the energy sends it, so the right placement of the oars is surely all you need to do to be able to row well. Or so I thought! Rowing is technical and more frustrating than I anticipated (when watching Olympians glide through the water), and is also more rewarding than many other sports I've undertaken, when it goes well. And my experience is it's been about flow. It's about finding the perfect balance between thinking about what you're doing, and not thinking too much about what you're doing. Too much concentration can upset the natural instinct. Not thinking about technique enough can have you capsizing! It was when the coach asked us to row with our eyes closed to get the purity of the feel of the water I understood how the balance of thinking about technique and not overthinking achieved flow. It was this optimal state of consciousness that combined the feeling of being at my best with performing at my best, and in this flow-state I was able to achieve superior performance.

Carol Dweck's work on mindset, referred to earlier in this book, offers an interesting dimension to flow. Dweck shares the view mindset plays an important part in the development of talent, citing research findings where exceptional people, from swimmers to musicians, didn't show their talents until they studied and applied themselves. So mindsets can be changed by learning new skills. Dweck cites Mozart's ten years of work before writing anything she describes as memorable. So does learning have to precede flow?

Of course our proposition here is we all have genius within ourselves, but it could be in the applying of a growth mindset our genius is released. This ability to learn develops with maturity and means there's less reliance solely on natural talents and we stay open to new ideas.

What about those who are identified early in life as "gifted"? Dweck suggests labelling people, in particular children, can have a harmful effect. The "gifted" or "exceptional" children can actually be hampered by the label, not living up to its expectations. So if you're labelled as talented, does this label hinder your progress to achieve flow more readily, more often? Does it make you less likely to try to achieve it because you think you've already got it?

I'm sure we can all think of friends at school who were high achievers, who seemed to put little effort into exams and passed with flying colours. How many of them have gone on to be high flyers in adult life? And how many of those who had to work hard, study hard, and not always get straight As have gone on to be high flyers in adult life? Is that about knowing how to achieve flow, perhaps?

When looking at athletes with a growth mindset, their focus is less on the winning itself and more on the process; they ignore the distractions and enjoy the challenge as much as the outcome. An athlete with a fixed mindset tends to focus on the winning and will force this to prove they're better than the competition. This leads to greater dejection when they don't win.

The Flow Genome Project, established by Steven Kotler and Jamie Wheal to map the genome of flow, gives the technical definition of flow as an "optimal state of consciousness where we feel our best and perform our best," describing the sensation of flow where every action, every decision, arises seamlessly from the last.

They suggest there are three things we need to know about flow:

1. It creates powerful intrinsic motivation by releasing the most addictive neurochemicals in our bodies.

2. It cuts the path to mastery (10,000 hours) in half and accelerates performance up to 500%.
3. People with the most flow in their lives are the happiest.

People who have flow create their world around it and hence can find the greatest happiness. In his HBR acticle, Kotler describes how the release of neurochemicals in the brain contributes to the main stages of flow. In flow, the brain releases 2 cocktail of norepinephrine, dopamine, endorphins, anandamide, and serotonin. Flow is one of the only times the brain produces these five chemicals simultaneously. Kotler goes on to suggest the flow-state is one of the "most pleasurable, meaningful and—literally—addictive experiences available." (ref https://hbr.org/2014/05/create-a-work-environment-that-fosters-flow)

At there Flow Genome Project Kotler Wheal explain how the neurochemicals contribute to flow. First, adrenaline ensures we are alert and paying attention. Then norepinephrine is released, the hormone responsible for concentration. After this, dopamine is released. This enhances pattern recognition; our brain starts telling us we're "onto something" at this point and to give it our attention. These two chemicals combined help us ignore distractions while speeding up the connections between ideas. Then endorphins are released. These are the "happy" chemicals that help us feel invincible. Next, anandamide is released, which plays a role in helping us make connections, prompting lateral thinking. Finally serotonin is released—the feel-good chemical.

This combination of neurochemistry and brainwave states gives us access to solutions we don't normally have access to in normal consciousness, enabling us to make connections we wouldn't otherwise see.

In his book. *The Rise of Superman,* Steven Kotler of the Flow Genome Project suggests flow is found not through a magical epiphany but through the progression of multiple steps, some of which come from within and some from external contributors such as training, technology, and learning from previous attempts. The training that goes in to achieving outstanding results is not just physical training but mental as well. Kotler suggests there are psychological and intellectual talents required to succeed, such as grit, fortitude, courage, creativity, resilience, cooperation, critical thinking, pattern recognition, high speed "hot" decision-making—and these are accessed while under extreme pressure.

The Flow Genome Project references great, well-known geniuses of their time: Einstein, Curie, Archimedes, Mozart, and Michael Jordan. But surely flow is available to us all? They talk about us all being able to say, "Wow, that's incredible, and I can," rather than "That's awesome and I could never." So what about the rest of us?

In a world where we are increasingly bombarded by information and stimulation, and flow is a state of total absorption, and we need flow to access our genius, we can see the challenge before us.

Note from Myles: The Flow Genome project and Kotler's book raise some concerns among team members. There are three principle concerns:

1. The conception of flow is almost exclusively concerned with high adrenalin activities that involve very high levels of risk, where people are putting their lives in danger, which gives an unbalanced picture of flow, and more importantly, does not refer to the problems that occur, such as depression, when flow becomes an addiction.
2. Some of what is presented by Kotler as science may be speculation rather than inaccurate, e.g., the idea that anandanamide enhances lateral thinking.
3. The presentation of flow as a genome is curious, to say the least, for a genome is the genetic material of an organism, which is different from the understanding of flow as a mental state as acknowledged by scientists and experts in the field such as Dweck and Csikszentmihalyi. On the other hand, the work of the Flow Genome Project has captured much interest, particularly in the US, and as such deserves mention in this book.

Identity and Enabling Genius

Ian Harrison

"Who am I?" "Why am I here?" These questions are common to all of humanity. Individuals' answers to these questions will be shaped by their unique blend of theistic and atheistic philosophies; by their social context, and by their education. These answers are often held with passion and differences can be the cause of abrasive interactions.

In some ways the debates that surround the subject of identity echo those of the "nature versus nurture" debate. Are we born with our identity or does it develop? Is my sense of identity an expression of my eternal soul or is it a social construct? Fortunately, it is not for this article to contemplate the existence or otherwise of an eternal soul.

In the 18th century, the Scottish philosopher David Hume outlined what became known as "bundle theory". Applied to the self, this theory suggests that the self is not an object in its own right, but rather a bundle of properties. What is more, there is no sense in which these properties are inherent in the self.

. . . I may venture to affirm of the rest of mankind, that they are nothing but a bundle or collection of different perceptions, which succeed each other with an inconceivable rapidity, and are in a perpetual flux and movement. (David Hume)

Julian Baggini develops bundle theory in his book, *The Ego Trick*. At the core of his argument is the idea that our sense of self is a trick played on us by our brains that make us feel like there is something more unified than actually exists. This is not to say that the self does not exist, but that it is a process not an unchanging entity. In this construct the self is both there to be discovered and there to be created.

Long before David Hume described bundle theory, Plato suggested a startlingly similar view of the world. Plato suggested that the highest form of reality existed as nonmaterial (though substantial) "forms" or "ideas". He considered these forms to be the perfect essence of the things we experience. Put another way, Plato suggested that there was a set of perfect ideals, or pure properties, that did not exist in material form but that combined to define the things we experience. A chair may take many forms and those forms may develop over time, but we recognize the chair as a chair because it shares a particular set of properties.

One of the ways we identify ourselves is through the series of labels that we learn to attach to ourselves. These complex, overlapping, and sometimes contradictory labels each carry with them a set of "norms" or "ideals". If I label myself as working class, that label carries with it an array of properties that will influence the choices I make, the expectations I have of myself and others. Most importantly, these "norms" shape the way I define myself.

The debate over whether or not there is a core self that is inherent to our individuality will go on, probably forever. On one level it is the realm of philosophers and theologians, and yet we cannot think about enabling unique individual genius without giving some thought to the matter of identity.

There are, I think, three statements with which most people would agree regarding our experience of identity. Each one of these is helpful in the context of enabling genius.

First, whichever view you hold regarding the nature of the self, each of us has a strong enough experience of identity to reach one of the most simple and the most profound statements possible: "I am." There is a me and I am unique. In whatever way my self is constructed, however much of myself exists at conception and to whatever extent I am shaped by psycho-social experiences—I am; and no one else is quite like me.

Second, and equally undeniably, I change. I am shaped by my experience of life and I express myself differently in different contexts.

Finally, whether or not science ever identifies a core self, I remain recognizable. That is to say that, as I change, develop, and grow there is a progressive consistency. If you were to meet a close friend after many years apart, you would perceive them to have changed greatly and yet you are almost certainly going to recognize certain traits of character from all those years ago.

I am. I change. I remain recognizable. Each of these statements has a value when seeking to enable unique individual genius.

The desire to achieve personal genius is a desire for change. That change may challenge some of the ways in which we have previously defined ourselves. It will inevitably bring new experiences that shape us and inform our sense of identity. All that said, enabling genius may begin, not with a desire to be different, but with a desire to be me. It turns out that there is genius in the ability to be yourself in the moment you now occupy.

In 1970 Arnold Beisser, professor of psychiatry at the University of California, drew together implications from the work of Frederick Perls to form what he called his "paradoxical theory of change".

Briefly stated, it is this: that change occurs when one becomes what he is, not when he tries to become what he is not. Change does not take place through a coercive attempt by the individual or by another person to change him, but it does take place if one takes the time and effort to be what he is—to be fully invested in his current positions. (Arnold Beisser)

In other words, when I want to be what I am not, I become resistant to change, but when I embrace what I am in this moment then I become open to change. The ability to occupy my identity in this moment enables me to interact with my environment in a way that enables transformation. Enabling genius may begin with simply being yourself and embracing yourself for everything you are in this moment.

This level of authenticity rules out any shallow understanding of what it is to be authentic. The most shallow definition of authenticity requires only a resemblance of something original. Enabling genius requires a more substantial authenticity. One useful definition of authenticity is:

Relating to or denoting an emotionally appropriate, significant, purposive, and responsible mode of human life.[1]

If we combine this definition with Beiser's thinking, then we understand authenticity to be an approach to life that is emotionally appropriate to whom you are in this moment. I would argue that when we can live in this way, we are far more able to understand our own significance, our purpose, and what it means to live responsibly. In this context, the point of reference to this responsibility is our own identity, it being a form of irresponsibility to live in denial of ourselves.

This being the case, enabling genius requires three key ingredients:

- Self-awareness
- Self-regulation
- Relational transparency

Self-awareness is, of course, a necessity if one is to live with any degree of authenticity. LeFrancois[2] breaks down self-awareness into three further ingredients:

- **Self-esteem** is the positive or negative way individuals view themselves. It also entails the desire to be held in high esteem by others.
- **Self-concept** is the concept that individuals have of themselves. Notions of self are often linked to individuals' beliefs about how others perceive them.
- **Self-actualization** is the process or act of becoming oneself, developing one's potential, achieving an awareness of one's identity, and fulfilling oneself.
- **Self-regulation** enables us to control our responses to external stimuli. It is the ability to both adapt and to remain true to oneself.

Finally, relational transparency is the ability to make your true self visible in your relationships. That is not to say one must be totally visible at all times, but that what is visible is true to your identity in that moment.

This brings us to consider the ways in which our identity expresses itself in the world. There are at least four interfaces through which we express ourselves:

- Our values
- Our sense of purpose
- Our personality
- Our strengths

None of these are set in concrete and all are subject to change. In enabling genius, all are worth exploring.

It may be helpful to distinguish between "purpose" and "cause". In my experience the two are often confused and the confusion can be unhelpful and potentially destructive. In the words of Aaron Hurst:

Seeking our purpose is about finding a direction, not a destination. That is, purpose is a verb, not a noun. We may never find one true calling, but we can understand the colour of our purpose, which can help us have much more meaningful careers and lives .... Purpose isn't a cause; it is an approach to work and serving others.[3]

Hurst helpfully identifies three elements of purpose:
- Who do you work to impact?
  - Individuals.
  - Society.
  - Organizations.
- Why do you do what you do?
  - To create harmony by trying to balance the scales in a world with so much inequality.
  - To build karma, because what goes around comes around.
- How do you create that impact?
  - By building communities.
  - By meeting the needs of individuals.
  - By building enabling structures and frameworks.
  - By getting a better understanding.

Before moving on, it is important to return to the thought that our identity is not an unchanging entity that sits at the core of our being. Even if such a core exists, we are subject to change. To believe that an individual has a predefined and unchanging purpose is full of pitfalls. Even using Aaron Hurst's broad-brush approach, our sense of purpose may change over time. This being the case, it is best to hold our sense of purpose in the same way we hold our identity. It is an expression of now and not a definition of the past or of the future.

Understanding ourselves and developing the ability to occupy our identity in any given moment is an important ingredient to enabling our unique individual genius.

In 2010 the Nobel-Prize-winning economist George A. Akerlof and his colleague Rachel E. Kranton published an introduction to a new concept in Behavioural economics. *"Identity Economics"*[4] suggests that our conception of whom we are and whom we want to be may be the single most influential factor in how we work, learn, spend, and save. Disturbingly, their work also shows that the way others perceive our identity can also be a crucial determining factor in our economic wellbeing.

Akerlof and Kranton propose that we each have an identity utility. They suggest that in any given situation individuals' motivation (utility) is dependent on the extent to which their own actions and the actions of others correspond to their sense of identity/self-image. Put another way, our ability to access our genius is greatly affected by the relationship between our actions and our social context and our sense of identity. This is most easily understood in the context of the workplace. When a person feels like an "insider" in the workplace and their work fits with their own sense of self, then they are likely to be far less interested in extrinsic rewards and have far greater willingness to put in discretionary effort. However, if they feel like an "outsider" in the workplace and/or their work seems at odds with their sense of self, then they are more likely to seek higher extrinsic rewards to compensate them for their sense of loss and are far less likely to offer discretionary effort.

Akerlof and Kranton outline studies that show similar dynamics in the context of education, race, and gender.
In the context of this book, "Identity Economics" leads to a number of key conclusions. Enabling genius requires:

- An ability to be ourselves in the moment.
- An ability to reconstruct the unhelpful labels by which we identify ourselves.
- An ability to filter the impact of the expectations of others on our sense of identity.
- The exploration of our sense of purpose.
- Focusing our attention and actions on things that align with our sense of identity.

Claude Steele and Joshua Aronson's research showed that almost anything that reminds you of a negative or restricting label will negatively affect your performance. Enabling genius must address the labels by which we identify ourselves.

In the same way, we must change the way people understand the concept of genius. For as long as it is defined in such a way that it can be used as a label applied to a small minority, it will act as a limitation on the vast majority of people who are capable of discovering their own unique genius.

In the end, enabling genius is about enabling the self to be all it can be, to excel in the moment, to find new expressions of self, to develop, to grow, and to change.

Notes

[1] http://www.oxforddictionaries.com/definition/english/authentic
1. Beiser, Arnold. "The paradoxical theory of change" 1970. http://www.gestalt.org/arnie.htm

[2] Definition of autheniticity: http://www.oxforddictionaries.com/definition/english/authentic

[3] LeFrancois, G., *The Lifespan*. (New York: Wadsworth, 1996)

[4] Aaron Hurst, The Purpose Economy (Elevate, 2014), 101

[5] George A. Akerlof, Rachel E. Kranton, *Identity Economics* (Princeton University Press, 2010)

[6] Cited in Carol S. Dweck, *Mindset* (Ballantine, 2006), 75

Identity and Disillusion

Maxim Belukhin

This part is not about how to become a genius in a particular area. This represents an opinion on how to avoid a disillusion after achieving the main goal in a particular area. As we can see, many people seem to be happy because they are successful in a chosen professional journey. In fact, many of them are not as happy as we think they are. In our executive coaching practice, we shaped an opinion on two main roots for such a possible disillusion.

1. The assumption that each person has only one possible true authentic self
2. Ignoring other facets of our own identity except the professional identity.

Root 1
The Assumption that Each Person Has Only One Possible True Authentic Self

Many of us are trying to find out our only "true self". The only one and the one we will have forever. I guess that there is a possible trap here. In our childhood, each of us had a dream to become someone. Usually our wishes changed with our age. For example, now I am happy that I have not become a bus driver, as I had wanted when

I was four. In addition, I am happy that I have not chosen music as my main occupation, as I wanted to when I was 16. All we can be definitely sure of is that our desired "true self" is not constant and changes with our age and experience.

Particularly acute issues arise for people who invested much in their careers and now feel a desire to drop it and switch to a different field. All those people can be divided into two groups, I suggest.

First group—people who do not know what area they should choose next. They know that they have their "true self", somewhere deep inside, but they need to reflect in order to shape it.

Second group—people who think they know what they want to do next. They think they know exactly their one true mission.

Experience tells us that usually there is one common thing among those groups. Both of them do not know exactly what the "true self" looks like (if it exists) until he or she tried, succeeded, and recognized it. Most of the people who think that they have their only one true self figured it out only by using their introspection to find an inner truth. This knowing leads them to the identification of the desired end goal. Some of them have devised and implemented an action plan to attain it. That approach Herminia Ibarra[1] [Cora Chaired Professor of Leadership and Learning, and Professor of Organizational Behaviour at Insead Business School] named as a "plan and implement approach". The trap is that their introspection can be too subjective, dependable on their family background, significant exterior opinions, and influenced by the current situation.

History repeats itself and we tend to construct our so-called "true self" from something we belong to—ethnicity, values, memories, attitudes, all the desires we have at the very moment but do not have at that instant. The appetite to gain that step is so strong that it does not let us see the detailed parts of that new role. After we take up the new role, we are going to miss yet again something else and/or be disillusioned by what that role turned out to be. The truth is that any job has things we like and do not like to do. Usually when we want to switch to another occupation, we cannot see the weaknesses of that choice. Therefore, the chances to end in frustration are high enough.

Herminia Ibarra suggests a safer approach: "Shaping and revealing the self through testing. Learning from direct experience to recombine old and new skills, interests, and ways of thinking about oneself and to create opportunities that correspond to that evolving self."[2] This approach is based on the idea that you can have millions of possible selves. All you need to do is to start a very committed journey through daring, safe investigations in which you can see what works for you. In turn, it is important to be aware of how you feel when we play a fake self. After the experiments, you can shape several possible selves and switch to one of them with far better chances of success and happiness.

Root 2
Focusing on the Professional Role and Ignoring Other Parts of One's Real Identity

There is a nice woman, 45 years old, sitting in front of me. She looks self-confident and shares her success story. We are in a coaching session in which we are able to identify areas for future development in her professional life. She is the only woman among top executives in her large company. After she described her experience, we moved to challenges and concerns she had faced in the professional arena. Suddenly she remembered a reflection from one of her friends. Then she added that the opinion of that person was very important to her at that particular moment. Something in her Behaviour slightly changed while she was sharing her thoughts. A shadow of sadness appeared on her face. Impulsively I asked how difficult it was to find anybody as strong as she was in her personal life. She has looked at me with eyes filled with suffering, acute pain without tears. It seemed she shrank into herself. "Yes," she whispered quietly. Then she paused. "Do you think I need to have a family?" she asked me after a minute or so.

During my career, I have asked many people in their mid-careers about their true self and how they envision it. The answers are typically: top-manager, freelancer, singer, entrepreneur, business coach, department head, painter, composer, and so on. Usually people tell me about occupations or a career. I have not heard a single answer like: a happy father, mother, wife, husband, friend, and so on. Are these points less important elements for us? Why always discussions around professional or career identity? Imagine an average graduate who wants to become a top manager. If you discuss future plans with him, well-rounded themes such as career, family, children, friends, wellbeing, and hobbies will be included. So where does he lose all the other pieces of his completed picture?

Let's look at the same graduate once again. The main problem for him after the graduation usually is to find a well-paid job. So he becomes a young specialist. He is happy for about half a year or so and then the next desire is to become a manager. The reason is obvious: the job is better paid and easier to complete from his point of view. He already identifies himself as a manager and even tries to behave as one. His ego shines in the light; he critically views other managers and believes that he was born to be a real manager in comparison with people who occasionally happened to hold those positions today. In his mind he thinks, "It is a natural job for me," and "It is a very strange thing that nobody has suggested me for this new position." Of course, he is definitely sure that he will be far more effective in this role than his predecessors were. He is the first one in the office in the morning and the last one to leave for home. He is young and has a strong enough character to have such a lifestyle and position. He promises himself that upon becoming a manager his long hours will cool down. The propelling desires drive the rising disillusion; the dream will end after getting a new position and encountering unexpected wake-up calls.

Then he reflects on the questions: a) should he quit the game and find something else; b) continue his robust career ambitions; or c) stay on an achieved cruising level. If he chooses the further growth option, he would usually have the same situation at all the stages. The growth will demand more and more time and energy. It can be a kind of a rush. Nothing except a rush exists when you are in a rush. If he is married, he does not see his family, spending all the time in the rush. If he has no spouse or children, nothing is going to change in this area. If he has friends, he forgets all the activities he shares with them. Hobbies at this point do not count unless they help his advancement. What will he have at the end of a day?

Let's look at three large groups of people: successful women, men, and celebrities.

Women

In 2002, Sylvia Ann Hewlett[3] distributed her study about women executives in the US. According to that survey, 49% of ultra-achieving career women (earning more than $100,000, aged 41–55) are childless and 33% of high-achieving career women (earning $55,000-$66,000 aged 41–55) are childless; 57% are unmarried. Sylvia admits that before the interview with some of these women she thought that:

Exhilaration and challenge of a megawatt career made it easy to opt out of motherhood. Nothing could be further from truth. When I surveyed these women about children, their sense of loss was palpable. Consider Lisa Polsky, who joined Morgan Stanley in 1995 as managing director after successful stints at Citibank and Bankers Trust; she managed to make it on Wall Street, the ultimate bastion of male market power. But when we met in 1999, our conversation focused on what she had missed. Polsky was 44 then, and her childbearing days were over. She said. 'What gnaws at me is that I always assumed I would have children. Somehow I imagined that having a child was something I would get in a year or so, after the next promotion, when I was more established.'

We can find many similar examples, which can make us feel that it is a common delusion. However, maybe young generations are wiser? Sylvia gives the example of a 29-year-old female lawyer, who told her that now the situation has changed, and it is not so difficult for women to have a career and postpone childbirth to a later period thanks to the progress in medicine. However, are we not going to repeat the same pattern?

Men

In the same article, Sylvia gives us information that the more successful a man is, the more likely to have a spouse and children. Only 19% of ultra-achieving men are childless and 17% unmarried. However, there is a very sad anecdote about a man who is immersed in his career.

Once a manager came home late. He found his four-year-old son awake. It was a surprise for him, because usually it was time for sleep. The son asked him how much money he earned per hour. The manager was annoyed and told to his son that he had been working through the whole day and was exhausted, wanted to have dinner and relax instead of answering foolish questions. But then he said, '$100 per hour.' After that, the son asked him for $20. The manager got angry and told his son that he was thinking only about getting money for himself and not about his tired father. He did not give him money and sent him to bed. But later the manager decided that his son might really need the money. He had never asked for it before. He came into his son's room and gave him money. The son seemed happy and put the money under the pillow with all his other bills. The manager was furious. 'Why did you beg for money when you already have some?' he asked. The son told him that he had only $180 and he needed $200. Then the son gave all of the money to his father. He told him that he had been missing him and he

*was going to pay him for coming home two hours earlier to have dinner
with him and his mother.*

The business literature is full of examples of managers who lost
their health, families, and all just because of career abuse. Most of
them wish they had spent more time with their families, parents,
and friends after they realized what they have lost. Not a single one
wished he had spent more time at work.

Celebrities

Celebrities are often role models for others and objects of envy.
They seem to be the happiest people in the world, who have found
a real "true self". They do the job they were born for, earning
enormously huge amounts of money. From another side, look at
how many of them ended up drug abusers, alcoholics, and victims
of suicide.

Conclusions

- A great number of professionally successful geniuses have
  immersed, but these people are not happy.
- The choice of total immersion into only one sphere of life was
  not their conscious decision. Many of them thought that their
  life was balanced, or would be balanced in future.
- To understand what is really important, some people need the
  real experience of losing it. In that moment of truth, all the secondary sides are discarded and the main theme takes it all. It can
  be too late!
- No one can be sure that the choice of area for dedicating all one's
  life to is the best one. So it is suggested that risk-sharing between
  various dimensions is wiser and investing in each and every one
  of them is safer. It is impossible to be a genius in all spheres of
  life, but you are to:

1. Select the most relevant and necessary areas and determine the minimum level of desired success in them. For example,

   - *Family—parents, children, siblings, in-laws, and so on*
   - *Social and community—friendship and community engagement*
   - *Spiritual—religion, philosophy, or emotional outlook*
   - *Physical—health and wellbeing*
   - *Material—physical environment and possessions*
   - *Vocational—hobbies and other non-professional activities*
   - *Career*

2. Evaluate the development of each dimension.

3. Compare two pictures—the desired one and the current one—to show the difference and help understand where one is at the present moment. What are the investment and opportunity costs for achieving the result? Almost every decision—whether agreeing with a strategic business alliance or committing to a leadership role in a non-profit organization—involves two kinds of costs. There's the investment cost: time, energy, and other resources expended. And there's the opportunity cost: the options you forgot by investing those resources. The challenge with investment costs is to be explicit about them up front and understand if and how incurring them will lead you to your desired, well-defined outcome.

4. Start experiments through trial and error.

Notes

[1] Herminia Ibarra *"Working Identity unconventional strategies for reinventing your career"* *(Harvard Business School Press Boston Massachusetts 2003,) 29-34*

[2] Herminia Ibarra *"Working Identity unconventional strategies for reinventing your career"* *(Harvard Business School Press Boston Massachusetts 2003), 39*

[3] Sylvia Ann Hewlett *"Executive Women and the Myth of Having It All"* ("Harvard Business Review" April 2002)

Mindset, Flow, and Genius

Sue Coyne and James Gairdner

Mindset: One of the Four Pillars of Enabling Genius

1. Our Intentions and Contentions

Mindset or *Directional knowledge is the orientation for practice. This kind of overarching knowledge includes cultural and disciplinary paradigms, social identities, stance, values, roles, and motivations. Directional knowledge is in large part tacit and deeply embedded. It rarely bears scrutiny, except in times of transformational change within a personal practice or practice community. Directional knowledge is quietly developed and is often taken for granted.*

Dr Hilary Austin

It is our contention that:

- Mindset is a critical enabler of an individual's ability to access genius;
- The greater the alignment between all the elements of mindset, the greater the likelihood that an individual can channel genius; and
- This struggle for alignment can be challenging, as many aspects of mindset are "deeply embedded" and often taken for granted.

The process of mindset alignment starts with a willingness to engage with a world in which what we see doesn't equal reality. But a mental construction, or a model if you will, which by definition tends to be an impoverished version of that which is really there. It requires a willingness to let go of concepts such as right and wrong and to recognize that societal pressures, our upbringing, and interactions with our external world can have us construe layers of identity that are incongruent with accessing genius.

We will set out our understanding of what it takes to create a mindset that is resonant with genius and that allows it to flow. In doing so, we draw on many different models and theories about mindset and its various components, as well as our own experience as human beings and coaches.

From the outset it is worth noting that we are as guilty as anyone else of having a subjective view of the world. So, where possible, we will identify where we have interpreted data and where we have not. Our intention in writing is to articulate a point of view with the hope of inspiration, discussion, exploration, and evolution of the collective understanding of the connection between mindset, flow, and genius.

2. Our Definition of Mindset

It's important to start with a definition of mindset. Mindset is: *the neural blueprint that creates our view of the world and our way of being in the world.*

Mindset is multi-layered, as shown in the diagram over the page. It is important to note that as we move from the outer layers toward the inner layers, we become less consciously aware of the fundamental drivers of our thoughts and Behaviours.

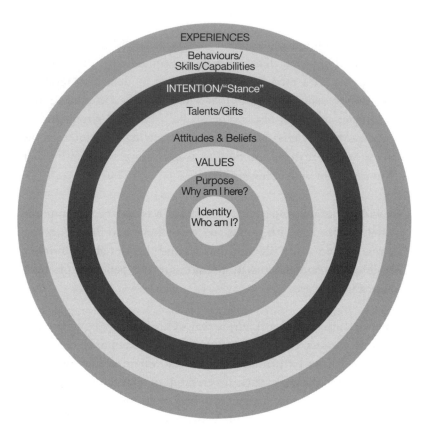

Starting from the center, the most unconscious parts of our mindset encompass:

- Identity—Who am I?
- Purpose—Why am I here?
- Values
- Attitudes and beliefs
- Talent/gifts

Much of these unconscious aspects of our mindset are hardwired during the first seven years of life, when our brains are like a sponge and take on the beliefs and attitudes of the adults and environment around us. There is a great body of work unfolding in the area of early education and mindset. Of note is the work by Lilian Katz, which focuses on the determination of attitudes and dispositions; of Malaguzzi (*Hundred Languages of Children*) on the link between environment and learning; of Ken Robinson (the most-watched TED video of all time, "Do Schools Kill Creativity?"); and of Stuart Brown ("Play," available on TED) on play and learning.

It is our contention that the collection of these layers forms what Roger Martin describes as our stance, which sits at the interface between our internal and external worlds. Stance, according to Martin, is made up of two components: "What is the nature of the world?" and "What is my role in the world?". So it is that our stance or intention is determined in large part by an identity, and a set of beliefs, attitudes and values of which, on a day-to-day basis, we are largely unaware.

This is important because it is our stance that influences the makeup of our outer mindset, our resultant Behaviours and outputs in the external world. By way of example, if you walk into a meeting expecting it to be hostile, you are likely to give off either defensive or aggressive signals regardless of what you say. This in turn will provoke a response and as you predicted, a confrontational interaction. As Sid Banks' "inside out" model suggests, "Our feelings are our thoughts unfolding in the moment." Shift your stance and see what feelings, thoughts, Behaviours, and ultimately outcomes you are able to achieve.

So mindset operates at three levels: inner, surface, and outer, with a dynamic but largely hidden interplay between these two inner two levels.

3. Journey to the Center of Mindset

The majority of us live our lives according to the default mindset acquired during our early years, unaware of the latest research in neuroscience and specifically a phenomenon called neuroplasticity, which suggests that we can update our default patterns to form new patterns of thoughts and actions in a similar way to the upgrading of software on a computer. If we stick with our default settings, we may find that they are often not appropriate for our own adult lives and result in suboptimal performance.

As we mature into adulthood, we develop our self-awareness through experience, learning, feedback, reflection, coaching, and sometimes therapy. This helps us evolve some of the outer layers, strengthening some aspects, deleting others, and adding new skills, capabilities, and Behavioural patterns to the mix. There has been much written about emotional intelligence in the last 20 years and developing our emotional intelligence may be the start of this journey, as self-aware-ness is a key element.

Often there is a realization that some of our Behaviours are not serv-ing us well and will not enable us to get the outcomes or the results that we want. We then learn that our thoughts and beliefs influence our emotions, which influence our Behaviours (based on cognitive Behavioural therapy[1]. So in order to change our Behaviour we need to change our thoughts and beliefs. At this stage we start to bring some of our unconscious, limiting beliefs to conscious awareness and set about hardwiring some alternative, more empowering beliefs.

Sometimes the journey of self-awareness takes us deeper into the unconscious mind and we start to become aware of our values and rules for living. Eventually some take this right to the core, to iden-tity and purpose.

The journey through these layers of the unconscious mind can be challenging, as it requires that we let go of our existing constructs, then undertake an inner exploration during which we are almost held in suspense, in a kind of limbo land, where we are no longer who we were but nor are we who we are becoming. During this period (think caterpillar and chrysalis), we can feel lost and anxious about not knowing what the future holds. It is all about allowing the new mindset to be put in place and then the new Behaviours and ways of operating in the world to emerge. Realising our potential and allowing genius to flow through us means that we will constantly be growing and evolving to ever-more developed levels of being or doing. Thus we go through this change—a transformation process on an on-going basis—and it is like a spiral. (explained in Theory U[2], developed by Otto Scharmer).

We advocate a dynamic and linear learning process where interactions between the individual and their environment (experiences) inform evolutions to outer (here called tools), surface (intention) and inner mindset (identity). This may look something like this: (borrowed from Roger Martin, *The Opposable Mind*[3])

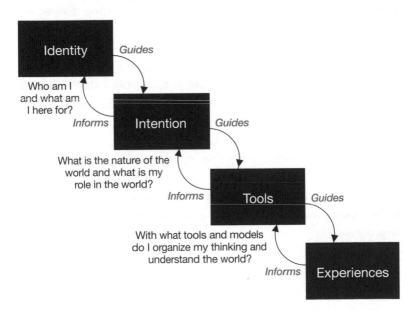

4. The Genius Mindset
Simply, a genius mindset occurs when there is complete alignment between outer, surface, and inner mindset—a state where there is no dissonance between layers and that creates the possibility for genius to flow. It is our contention that just as "interference" adversely impacts the ability of individuals to express their full potential, the

dissonance between layers interrupts the flow of genius and the expression of genius in our context.

So:
Expression = Genius - Dissonance

5. Creating Resonance

Therefore, achieving the expression of genius can require a fundamental rewiring of our mindset. As we have said, neuroscience has shown us that our brains have plasticity, which enables this rewiring to take place. In fact, if we had the equipment we could even observe those changes taking place. The key, if we are willing, is to understand which aspects of our mindset are creating dissonance and rewire them for resonance.

Carol Dweck, a thought leader in this area, gave us a key distinction with regard to mindset. She refers to having either a growth or a fixed mindset. Several neurological studies have shown that there is a fundamental difference in the brain processing of these two states. A fixed mindset results in a focus on outputs and solutions and a fixation on finding the "right" answer. A growth mindset is focused on gaining a deeper understanding of the mystery at hand and being happy to wade into the problem without automatically seeking resolution. It is also about seeing yourself as a "work in progress".

The growth mindset is clearly a prerequisite for enabling genius, but why is this important?

As we have said, our contention is that what enables genius to flow is resonance between the different layers making up our mindset. Having a growth mindset is a key enabler of this state of resonance. A fixed mindset creates dissonance and prevents the flow of genius. (For the older reader, think *Dark Side of the Moon* album cover.)

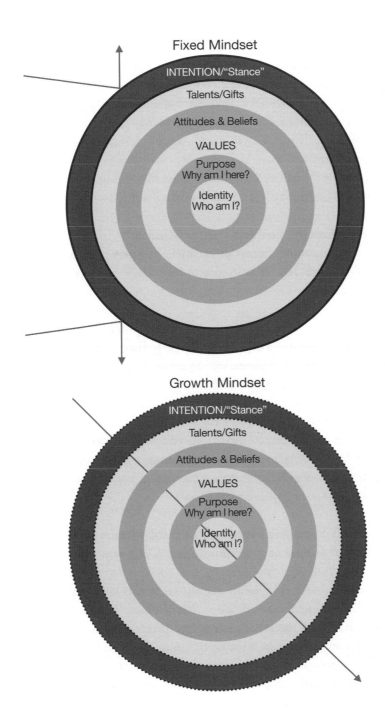

Our conscious "outer" mindset can also create dissonance. For example, it creates fear of the unknown and a need to control, which stops us from growing. It undermines our confidence by saying things like, "I can't do this" or "Who am I to have this big purpose?" Alternatively it might suggest that if we develop and grow, we may no longer fit in with our social group. It acts as a critic and naysayer instead of supporting and encouraging us to grow. Very often the conscious mind has us busy thinking about the past and the future rather than being present in the moment and in this way it keeps us distracted and unaware.

6. So How Can We Enable a Genius Mindset?

If the conscious mind creates dissonance, in order to create a resonant genius mindset, it is useful to find ways of bypassing the conscious mind.

Our belief is that there are two ways to avoid potential dissonance from the conscious mind that are rarely used. They occur at the level of stance in the initial diagram, and create an additional connection between the inner and outer world.

The first is setting an intention for something to happen. In this instance you would set an intention, which gives permission for genius to flow. Setting an intention sets things in motion because, as has been shown in quantum science, everything is energy and where you focus your attention energy follows[4].

The second is developing a practice that enables you to access a state of being such as flow or mindfulness that allows you to access the energy of genius once it is flowing and apply it to your being or doing. Mindfulness and flow are not the same, but both require you to be fully present in the moment. Mindfulness has been shown by research to be a means of getting into flow[5]. On the journey of developing self-awareness, dissonance can occur at each layer of the mindset. Interventions can therefore be made at any of these levels to manage the dissonance and create a resonant genius mindset.

Examples:

- Behaviour—reactive Behaviour due to the stress response, resulting in fight/flight/freeze. Identifying the triggers and learning to manage them through breathing or staying present can change this. Identifying early signs before the stress response is triggered and interrupting them is also effective.
- Emotions—developing emotional intelligence so you can recognize your own emotions and manage them. The next step then is to learn to recognize emotions in others and adjust how you respond.
- Beliefs—use of psychology, psychotherapy, or coaching to surface limiting beliefs and then a process of identifying more appropriate, empowering beliefs that are resonant with your goals and hardwiring them using focus, attention, and repetition (the brain is receptive when in a theta state so in theory hypnosis should also be a possible route for hardwiring new beliefs). There is also new evidence that brain entrainment— sounds and rhythms at certain frequencies—can put the brain into a receptive state and help with hardwiring new beliefs. Developing a growth mindset rather than a fixed mindset with regard to learning is a key aspect of the sort of beliefs that support genius.
- Somatic—cognitive interventions where the physiology is changed and that then starts to change the feelings and beliefs (i.e., it works in the opposite way as that described under beliefs). This could include play or acting "as if".
- Values elicitation—using exercises to help elicit unconscious values.
- Doing deep work to identify who you are and what you stand for and also purpose, why you are here. Personal brand is a good vehicle for this (personal branding is the practice of people branding themselves and their careers).
- Intention—consciously setting intentions aligned with your desired outcomes.

As advocated in the work of Richard Sennet on craft and "marrying of head, heart and hands," awareness can be further developed by daily practise of mindfulness, meditation, achieving autonomic balance[6], and exercises to enable accessing flow at will. It would also include the ability to manage your frequency and energy field and connect up to the wider energy field[7].

Notes

[1] Cognitive Behavioural Therapy, or CBT, aims to help people become aware of negative thinking patterns and the Behavioural patterns that result and to develop alternative ways of thinking and behaving that are more positive. Two of the earliest forms of cognitive Behavioural therapy were Rational Emotive Behaviour Therapy (REBT), developed by Albert Ellis in the 1950s, and Cognitive Therapy, developed by Aaron T. Beck in the 1960s.

[2] Otto C Scharmer, *Theory U: Leading from the Future as It Emerges.* (San Francisco: Berrett-Koehler Publishers Inc, 2009)

[3] Roger Martin, *The Opposable Mind: How Successful Leaders Win Through Integrative Thinking* (Boston: Harvard Business Press, 2007)

[4] Quantum Physics Heisenberg Particle and Wave theory and Double slit experiment.

[5] Y. H.Kee & John C. K. Wang, "Relationships between mindfulness, flow dispositions and mental skills adoption: A cluster analytic approach" *Psychology of Sport and Exercise* Vol.9 Issue.4 (2008): 393-411.

[6] Grant Soosalu & Marvin Oka, *M-braining. Using your Multiple Brains to do Cool Stuff* (London, Mbit International Pty Ltd, 2012)

[7] Quantum Science: everything is energy and all energy is interconnected.

Teams and Collective Genius

Andrei Mikhaylenko and Lena Sobel

Most of what we know about flow lies within our individual experience. We are aware about conditions of flow and its benefits for us as individuals. But is it possible to get the same effect for a team to enable its collective genius? Can the whole team experience the same degree of complete involvement, clarity of what needs to be done, and self-realization that a teammate does? At the very moment when we are enjoying the Rolling Stones' live show, we have to admit that the band at least looks as if they can do it. And they look so for more than 50 years of their life as a group.

Andrei, a co-author of this article, has seen something like this in the office of Jodric, a small creative studio in Ho Chi Minh City, Vietnam. The founders of the company, Dung Ngo and Tri Lam, along with about a dozen other members of their team, were loitering around their spacious office—from workstations to the coffee maker, and on to the snooker table, and farther to the meeting room with glass walls. It looked as if they were doing nothing special, but at the same time I realized that right before my very eyes the big ideas for an on-going project in the banking sector appeared, one after another. It was a very important project for them, the deadlines were tight, but the guys were doing their job cheerfully and with no sign of effort. And as Dung said later, they had done it so for more than 13 years of their life as a company. A high-performance team needs to be in flow, the state where the individuals are fully immersed in a feeling of energized focus, full involvement, and enjoyment in the process of the activity. A team in flow can be characterized by the ease and sense of fulfilment and purpose that the participants enjoy, as well as a perfect notion of goals and purpose. Problems are there to be solved and new ideas keep emerging. In the state of flow, everything seems possible. Teams achieve results with fewer resources, time, money, and people than everyone thought possible, the team members included. Individuals build on each other's ideas and contributions and are more or less single-minded in the pursuit of solutions and results, and at the same time open to contributions from other teammates.

Certainly neither the band nor Jodric called themselves a "team in flow". They probably were not even aware of this concept. But they both conform to this. We can find many other examples of teams at work looking similarly—not only in the entertainment or visual design industry. What does make them different?

Layers of Flow

The whole is greater than the sum of its parts. These words, often attributed to Aristotle, may be considered as the basis for the whole concept of teamwork, including the idea of team in flow as a part of it. Let us paraphrase it in the way that "the whole creates the flow that the sum of its parts cannot make." It sounds no less true than the Greek philosopher's dictum. Then we can assume that a team in flow has at least two layers: first, the multitude of individual flows (the "sum"), and second, the overarching "whole"—the shared flow.

And here the "greatness" of the whole comes. The shared flow, which also may be described as "synergy effect", creates an extra value for each teammate and enriches everyone's flow to a degree that is not reachable individually. As one of my coaching clients mentioned (while answering my question on why he accepted the offer to be the leader of what he called the "mission impossible" project), "Each of us said it was impossible, but when we gathered all our *impossibles* together, we should admit that, well, it was possible if we would be in charge of it."

It is not clear what comes first among the individual flows and shared flows. In some cases a single personal flow can set light to the group inspiration and flow-like actions. Here we can recall hundreds of stories about visionary leaders. On the other hand, a strongly shared flow can completely reconfigure an individual flow or create it from scratch.

Lino Pazo Pampillon, a coach from Spain and our colleague on the Enabling Genius project, finds it very understandable in light of the mirror neurons' theory. The theory is based on a series of scientific observations showing that certain brain regions are active not only when people experience an emotion, but also when they see another person experiencing the same emotion. A subset of neurons from the brain region mirrors the emotion, performing a virtual reality simulation of the mind[1]. We are social animals, says Lino, and if a person on a team has a real passion about a certain thing, it can spread without hindrance across the whole group.

In the early 1990s, Andrei, as the marketing manager, joined the team of Will Bob, an American serving as deputy CEO for Delta Telecom, a company pioneering the Russian mobile telephony market. He could hardly believe that mobile telephony would hold his interest for more than a few months. He thought he just needed it for a while, before he was able to find a more appropriate job (he graduated from university with a degree in psychology). But it took a little bit longer than he assumed—some 15 years, during which he was climbing up the ranks in the world of telecommunications. Why? Because of his first year with Will. He was dramatically captured by the crazy idea of the multicultural team to build a new, wonderful wireless world, a fantastic place with borderless reachability (which many of us see as a big inconvenience now)! That was his first team in flow, as he now realizes. Interestingly enough, in 1992, the year of peak performance for the Delta Telecom team, none of them even heard about the book written just two years before, *Flow: The Psychology of Optimal Experience*[2].

What we believe in is that both layers of flow are necessary to create a team in flow. As a member of a team, no one is able to deliberately switch from the individual flow to the shared one, like we can do while switching our camera from photo mode to video mode. Being a part of series of enthralling business trips (sometimes they were to make a dozen of five- to nine-hour nonstop flights over a month, crossing Russia from west to east to visit each of our branches), Andrei was definitely enjoying the roaring shared flow of the team. But between trips, in the quiet of the office, when he was drafting a promo campaign for the bestselling first portable mobile phone (a bit more than 1 kg of weight), he was very much inside of his own flow, as copywriting and creative marketing were his real passion. It was his wonderland, where the time went differently, and where he was the very Alice.

As a team member, one constantly migrates from the individual flow to the shared one—sometimes in a barely perceptible way. Today, in the midst of the team brainstorming session at Zest Leaders, the company where Andrei is a partner, he can be completely taken by the shared flow. But three hours later he may be found making preparations (alone or in a small group) for a new challenging project and deeply in his personal flow, which is orchestrated by his unique abilities or interests. He can experience flow, but he can hardly distinguish between the "layers" of it. This is all about the concentration, excitement, and enjoyment, fused into a single flow. Can the shared flow exist without individual flows? We doubt so. The "own" flow is a root, while the team's common flow is the tree.

The less roots, the dryer the tree. No roots, no tree. Can the individual flows survive with no team flow around them? Of course, though with some transformations. John, Paul, and George, as well as Ringo—each of them remained (or still remain) in their own flow for quite a long time after the Beatles' breakup. "There's nothing you can do that can't be done ... It is easy ... " Indeed, flow is all we need.

Models of Teams in Flow

The idea of team in flow resides in the neighbourhood of many other similar models. One is the concept of self-managed teams. According to this approach, teams with minimal authority (in which team members have responsibility only for actually executing the task) represent "manager-led" teams. The more authority a team has, the more functions it fulfils, gradually becoming a self-managing, self-designing, and finally self-governing team[3]. Self-governing teams, besides executing tasks, are also responsible for managing their own work processes, designing itself as a team, and setting its overall direction.

Individual flows have more chance to survive and grow within teams where there is a significant amount of authority (or self-management capacity). In such teams, less impacts from the outside corporate world can impose limitations on the team members' flows. Because of this, the flows can amplify each other and bring to the team synergy and agility that never could be enforced by a leader or an organizational context itself.

Another similar model is the "internal work motivation" by Greg Oldham and Richard Hackman. They approached the problem of satisfaction with work from the side of job design. The researchers revealed that such "core job characteristics" as task variety, task significance, autonomy, and feedback cause certain "psychological states" of employees: experienced meaningfulness of work, and responsibility of work outcome, as well as knowledge of results from work activities.

Oldham's and Hackman's findings have been extensively used by consulting practitioners and managers to lower absenteeism and turnover at work. They developed their Job Characteristics Theory (JCT)[4], targeted to finding new sources of internal motivation for employees, in 1975, the same year Csikszentmihalyi published his first book on the very close topic, *Beyond Boredom and Anxiety: Experiencing Flow in Work and Play*. So at least 40 years passed since the virtual team of researchers, including Csikszentmihalyi, Oldham, Hackman, and many other prominent names, started a journey in search of the optimal combination of organizational efficacy and people's happiness at work.

Another person who has studied high performance teams is Susan Wheelan, a former professor at Temple University, in Philadelphia. She has studied development of groups for over 30 years, and made meta-studies from a group perspective. According to her findings, groups develop in a predictable manner. From level one, which can be characterized as "child," to level two "teenager," through to level three "young adult" and to level four "mature adult". In level four, you find high performance teams, or teams in flow. In this stage, a team uses most of its energy for production and its task. It is characterized by intensive and efficient cooperation toward a common goal. Not every group reaches level four, or even level three. To do so, you have to work with goals, relations, and results. She has also created a tool that measures the group's level, the Group Dynamic Questionnaire (GDQ). According to Susan Wheelan, it takes time to reach levels three and four; normally it can take up to one to two months for each level.

In late 2000, Keith Sawyer adapted the concept of individual flow to explain how innovation can be boosted through creating improvisational, emergent, and fluid teams[5]. Putting together results of research with groups as diverse as corporate teams, jazz orchestras, improvisational theatre ensembles, and sports teams, he found a range of conditions that enables group flow:

- Shared goals;
- Deep listening to each other;
- Complete concentration;
- Being able to control the group's actions;
- Blending of individual egos;
- Equal participation;
- Members' familiarity with each other;
- Constant communication;
- Elaboration of each others' ideas; and
- Learning from failure.

Sawyer is an evangelist of "group genius", as he strongly believes that innovation always emerges from a series of sparks, and it never comes out of a single flash of an individual genius.

One of the more recent insights on the teams in flow was the "sand dune teams" theory, a brainchild of Richard Hackman. He started developing the concept a few years before his passing in 2013 and left it unfinished. The sand dune teams, according to Hackman, are "Dynamic social systems that have fluid rather than fixed composition and boundaries. Just as sand dunes change in number and shape as winds change, teams of various sizes and kinds form and reform within a larger organizational unit as external demands and requirements change."[6] The concept of the "social sand dunes" having the capacity to gradually reshape themselves echoes a central idea of self-governing teams—being an effective solution for modern fast-changing contexts.

Flow for a sand dune team is not only its inner intent and way of engaging its teammates in a shared agenda, but also a way of forming the team's structure and composition. Sand dune teams operate in flow in its both inner (motivation, energy) and outer (size, composition, boundaries) dimensions. It provides, due to its outer transformability, more options for an individual in finding an optimal role within the team (or outside of it, what in turn is ultimately good for an individual flow). People with no significant roles, as well as dormant functions, do not survive there. At the same time, any dune has a less-changeable bed inside that is people with a mission to stabilize the dune in the mutable landscape and make the team flow on-going.

How to Build a Team in Flow

Flow is fragile. Both for individuals and groups, it appears from within, sometimes without any apparent reason. It can hardly result from a firm decision to have it. Moreover, the existing flow may dissolve as one tries to dig in and scrutinize its anatomy. Enjoying playing basketball, having a mystical experience, or losing track of time in debates with your new start-up team—your immersion in that fades as somebody tries to approach you with the question of what makes you feel like that.

Does it mean that we cannot deliberately build the flow? It does not look so. If you balance your intuitive sensitivity to its fragility and awareness about the group flow's fundamentals, you will have more chances for at least a clear direction for the emerging team flow. We assume that you as a reader of this book have already taken place as a flow enabler or are interested in becoming one. While considering your needs in building or further developing the flow capacity for your team, you may refer to the following checklist that summarizes the key findings about teams in flow, divided into the categories of individual qualities, prerequisites for the team, and qualities of the team as a whole:

	Team Flow Drivers	Self-Check Questions	Notes
	Individual Qualities of Teammates		
1	**Flow enabler(s)** The team includes people committed to enabling flow for the whole group.	- Am I a person committed to enabling conditions of flow for my team? Who else in the team is interested in that? - What outcome would I (and the other enablers) like from turning us into a team in flow? - How important is our purpose for me? How can we make it even more important? - How interesting and challenging are our goals?	
2	**Noticeable flows at an individual level** Each teammate is in flow, the shared or personal one.	- Can I see signs of flow from each member of the team? - What can I do to enable flow for those teammates who do not have it yet? (purpose, engagement, relationships)	

3	**Core of the team** There is a group of people in the team that are stable over time; these people are able to sustain the team flow and carry it forward.	- Is there a core of the team? - Who makes the core? - How can I encourage them?	
Prerequisites for the Team [1]			
4	**Small number** Small enough to let its members easily meet, communicate, be open and produce.	- Is it easy to meet? - Is there space for everyone to talk and be heard? - Are our discussions open and honest? - Does everyone know everyone else and their skills and roles?	
5	**Complementary skills** Do the teammates have the required skills, knowledge, network, and competences required?	- What potentials do each and every teammate have? - What competences are critical? - What do we need to learn?	

Note

[1] Jon R. Katzenbach, Douglas K. Smith, *The Wisdom of Teams: Creating the High-Perfomance Organization* (New York: HarperCollins Publishers Inc. 1993. Mcgraw-Hill Professional 2005, Harvard Business Review Press 2015)

| 6 | **Committed to a common purpose** Is there a meaningful purpose for *each and every team member?* | - How committed is everyone? What could increase our commitment?
- Is the purpose something larger than short-sighted goals?
- Does everyone on the team understand the purpose? And are we able to explain it to others?
- Do they understand the same thing? Or do they have different ideas?
- Do we talk about the purpose within the team and with people outside?
- Can you remember the purpose? | |
| 7 | **Committed to common goals** Goals for the team—not the organization or individuals. | - Can you remember the goals?
- Are they simple and measurable?
- Challenging? | |

8	**Common approach** Have you agreed upon an approach and how to work?	- Do you agree on the work approach? - Will your approach give you the opportunity to learn and grow as individuals and as a team? - How do you manage time?	
9	**Hold each other mutually accountable** I, or the team, have not succeeded if one of my teammates fail.	- Is the team both individually and collectively responsible for results, goals, and work approach? - Is there a feeling of "only the team can fail"- not individuals?	

Qualities of the Team as a Whole

10	**Awareness about the team's identity** Everyone on the team can give his or her own version of the team's unique traits; some of these traits are displayed by most of the team members.	- What are the unique traits of the team? What makes us different? - Which of these unique traits do the team members like most of all?	

11	**Team learning** The teammates learn from each other, as well as from the task at hand; the team is fluid and agile enough to be able to absorb new competences and fulfil more complex and challenging tasks.	- What have we recently learned as a team? What new team competences have we developed? - What exactly has each of us learned while working on the team? What new experience has each team member had?	
12	**Self-management capacity of the team** The team has a great extent of authority and self-management capacity.	- Can the team make decisions on its work processes and change them? - Can the team decide on its structure and composition? Can we make internal firing and hiring decisions ourselves? - Can the team set its overall direction itself?	

To be a part of a team is a great experience. But being a part of a team in flow can make a difference. Having tried this once, we are unlikely to want to go back to working within a "normal team". It is not because teams with the collective genius perform better than others, but rather because working in flow allows us to better understand who we are and be happier human beings. And because of this, any desired results are much more likely to happen.

Notes

[1] Interview with V.S. Ramachandran by Jason March. "Do Mirror Neurons Give Us Empathy?"
http://greatergood.berkeley.edu/article/item/do_mirror_neurons_give_empathy

[2] Mihaly Csikszentmihalyi, *Flow: The Psychology of Optimal Experience* (New York: Harper & Row, 1990).

[3] J. Richard Hackman, *Leading Teams: Setting the Stage for Great Performances* (Boston: Harvard Business Scholl Press, 2002), 52-53

[4] Hackman, J. Richard; Oldham, Greg R., "Development of the Job Diagnostic Survey", *Journal of Applied Psychology, Vol .60(2) (April 1975): 159-170.*

[5] Susan Wheelan, *Creating Effective Teams* (SAGE Publications Inc, 2014)

[6] Keith Sawyer, *Group genius: The Creative Power of Collaboration* (New York: Basic Books, 2007)

[7] J. Richard Hackman, Anita Williams Woolley, "Creating and Leading Analytic Teams". Tepper School of Business, Carnegie Mellon University, Research Showcase @ CMU (8-2008): 13
http://repository.cmu.edu/cgi/viewcontent.cgi?article=2502&context=tepper

Afterword

As you will have seen, Enabling Genius has proven to be a simply enormous topic with so many facets and with so many ways of looking at it. Our approach has been to pull together the best research and thinking around excellence, to simplify it and communicate it as well as possible. The intention at the heart of this book is to create a new meaning for "genius" in the belief that thinking of genius as the preserve of the few is a collective, limiting belief that does not serve any of us. And we wanted to go beyond the notion of potential, because that idea has lost its impact, and get to something more challenging, more provocative in the belief that, in the 21st century, the problems we face and the opportunities that are present can only be overcome and taken advantage of by a step change in human performance, individually and collectively.

Our new meaning for genius we expressed as a series of propositions:
1. Genius is available to all.
2. Each person can develop a unique individual genius.
3. Each person can develop genius in any discipline, craft, or skill.
4. Moments of genius are available to all.
5. People can work together in a state of collective genius (which was not explored fully in this book).

We also developed the pillars of Enabling Genius. Again, this is not the whole story but, we believe, gets to the heart of enabling genius in a practical and applicable manner. Identity, mindset, desire and, in the center, learning – it's a process, remember.

During the course of writing my personal Enabling Genius project and genius laboratory, returning to competitive tennis took steps forward and backward. I lost the best part of a year due to injury;

steroid injections caused damage to the vision in my right eye, and I had arthroscopic surgery to my right hip. Nevertheless, in September 2016 I was accepted to play in an ITF (International Tennis Federation) for veterans (55 years and over) in Woking, just outside London. This was my first competitive match in 30 years. I lost in a fairly close match. The most important thing I took from the experience was confirmation, if that was needed, of the idea of unique individual genius. Clarity about my tennis genius and, from that, how I play provided a focus and structure to my approach and allowed me to persevere in the early stages of the match when doubt could have been crippling. All the learning was invaluable and will set the course for development over the winter—it's a process.

The Enabling Genius Project is, in its own way, a process too. Phase one has resulted in this book. The project team is meeting at the end of October 2015, which at the time of writing is four weeks away, to think about phase two. The project will continue and, I hope, involve many more people from a greater variety of disciplines. I invite you to join us; you will find us at www.enabling-genius.com

1   >>>>DO YOU THINK IT WOULD BE GOOD TO ADD SUM TAKEAWAYS HERE – JUST A WAY TO SUM UP OR END THE BOOK WITH SOME THOUGHTS<<<<

2   >>>>I THINK IT WOULD BE HELPFUL TO HAVE A LIST OF THE BOOKS AND ARTICLES THAT HAVE BEEN REFERrED TO – IF THE READER WANTS TO DO MORE RESEARCH –ITS EASIER TO HAVE ALL OF THESE IN ONE PLACE.<<<<<

An introduction to
Myles Downey

Myles Downey is a writer, speaker, consultant, and innovator and is widely regarded as one of the leading business coaches in Europe.

For more than 25 years, he has coached senior executives and leadership teams in some of the most prestigious organizations around the globe, enabling them to achieve extraordinary goals. In 1996, Myles founded The School of Coaching, and later, in 2015, The School of Coaching International to bring his coaching expertise in developing excellence to a wider global audience. He also created the first and only online coaching system, Enable, which extends high quality coaching to all in a flexible and affordable manner.

His book, *Effective Coaching,* sold 300,000 copies and is considered a seminal work on coaching. This was followed by *Effective Modern Coaching* in 2014. From 2013 to 2015, he led the international Enabling Genius Research Project, resulting in this book. The project continues to explore what it takes to make manifest excellence and genius.

Co-authors

Maxim Belukhin

Maxim Belukhin, an executive individual and team coach, has designed an approach to help organizations and individuals resolve their business issues through self-development. Maxim is a partner in several famous global leadership development institutions.

Sue Coyne

Sue Coyne, PCC, is a leadership and team coach and creator of the Effective Leadership Launcher online blended coaching programme. Sue is passionate about supporting leaders in enabling genius to flow through their organizations. She models this by enabling genius to flow in her own life.

Caroline Cryer

Caroline Cryer, BA Joint Hons, MSc Occupational Psychology, MSc Coaching and Behaviour Change, is a leadership development specialist who has worked in large, global organisations designing and delivering game-changing learning and leadership development agendas. She is driven by a passion and purpose to enable people to have the opportunity and choice to be the best they can be, in whatever their chosen field.

Tamara Cutrín Millán

After obtaining her degree in education, Tamara focused her professional career in emotional intelligence and coaching (personal, team, and executive). After achieving her skills as a coach, Tamara has focused her energies toward research into the neuroscience field. Tamara has just completed a Masters Degree in Neuroscience at the University of Santiago de Compostela.

James Gairdner

James is director of James Gairdner Associates, a design-led organisation and provider of transformational leadership programmes focused on identifying the glitches in our thinking and thus creating dramatic shifts in self-awareness, decision-making, creativity, and radical collaboration.

Ian Harrison

Ian Harrison's work is increasingly focused on the way identity and purpose, both shared and individual, impact the performance of organisations and their employees. For two years Ian curated the speakers programme for TEDxBrum. He splits his time between working with businesses and arts organisations. Ian is the director of Aspire Programs Ltd.

Richard Merrick

Richard has been a student of performance from his early career in the Royal Air Force, through a successful career in business, to his current work as a mentor and coach to new business ventures. At the heart of his approach is a relentless focus on the individual, mindsets, and innate capabilities more than qualification, and the identification and leverage of what we have come to describe as individual genius. He is a founder and director of GrowHouse Initiative Ltd, and lives with his wife, an authority on early education and inquiry, in rural Derbyshire.

Andrei Mikhailenko

Andrei Mikhailenko is a coach and partner in Zest Leaders, an international consulting group helping people and organisations go through critical changes in their lives. Zest Leaders is headquartered in St. Petersburg, Russia, and operates in Europe, Southeast Asia, and South Africa. Andrei, with his particular interest in the transformative power of the inner genius concept, joined the Enabling Genius project in 2013.

Irena O'Brien

Irena O'Brien is a cognitive neuroscientist, neurosemantic trainer and meta-coach. She is the founder and director of The Neuroscience School, providing neuroscience education for coaches, therapists, and health and wellness professionals. She uses her meta-coaching skills and neuroscience knowledge to support entrepreneurs, business professionals, and executives to create flow in their business and personal lives. Based in Montreal, Canada, Irena teaches students and coaches clients from around the world. Following her first career as a chartered accountant, she went on to obtain her PhD in psychology, specializing in cognitive neuroscience. Irena is passionate about flow and neuroscience and reads and writes about these topics extensively. She is especially skilled at turning insights from psychology and neuroscience into actionable tools to help business professionals unleash their genius.

Lino Pazó Pampillón

Lino Pazó Pampillón, born in Vigo, Spain, is a professional coach and mindfulness consultant. Lino has worked in a number of management positions in various automotive companies over the last twenty-five years and spent the last six years as business excellence manager in a global automotive company. An eternal apprentice, he is always trying to develop his own genius and help individuals, multicultural and multi-functional teams develop theirs. "The sooner we decide look inside ourselves, the less energy we spend rubbing lamps searching for a genius."

Lena Sobel

Lena Sobel, MSc and ACC, is the creator of Leadership for Informal Leaders and Leadership for Technical Specialists. Author of two bestselling books in Swedish, translated, *The Mentor—a Practical Guide* and *The Manager as Coach*. Lena is passionate about enabling genius in people, teams, and workflows.

Craig Walker

After working in marketing for L'Oreal in London and Paris, Craig moved to Spain to study performance tennis training methods. Craig now brings a holistic approach to high-performance tennis and strength and conditioning coaching in London.

Simon Williams

Simon Williams is the owner and co-founder of DMW, a technology consultancy that has been in operation for twenty-five years. He is a transformation leader with experience of growing SMEs and running major change programs for both public and private sector clients. Simon now focuses on leadership and team development, creating challenging, stimulating work environments. As a qualified executive coach, he realized the field lacked a convincing scientific approach and eagerly joined the Enabling Genius team to help develop the concept. Outside work he crawls over mountain passes on his bike and murders indie tunes on his guitar.

Contact details for all of the Enabling Genius co-authors can be found at www.enabling-genius.com.